COME DANCE WITH ME

THE ROYAL BALLET SCHOOL WHITE LODGE, RICHMOND

COME DANCE WITH ME

A MEMOIR
1898-1956

BY

NINETTE DE VALOIS

ILLUSTRATED

DANCE BOOKS LTD
9 CECIL COURT LONDON WC2

This edition first published in 1973
by Dance Books Ltd,
9 Cecil Court, London WC2N 4EZ
Reprinted in 1981
Printed in Great Britain
by Lowe & Brydone, Leeds
This is an unabridged republication of the edition first
published in 1957

© 1981 by Ninette de Valois

ISBN 0 903102 02 1

FOR

DAME MARGOT FONTEYN

AND

FREDERICK ASHTON C.B.E

WITH THE AUTHOR'S GRATITUDE

CONTENTS

LIST OF ILLUSTRATIONS

I am of Ireland,
And the Holy Land of Ireland,
"And time runs on," cried she.
"Come out of charity,
"Come dance with me in Ireland."

W. B. YEATS

INTRODUCTION

MANY friends suggested that I should take four months' leave of absence to write this book. That would have been very pleasant; the book, though, would never have been written. It has been said that I am an indefatigable collector of discomfort and difficulty; certainly my mind prefers adversity and complexity to any state of smooth living. Thus, time and again, the throb and upheaval of my travels by every form of locomotion on land, sea and in the air, has been for me the perfect background music.

I would emphasise that these writings are, in effect, just an attempt to tell a story. The story, however, is not concerned with somebody's private life: it is just a glimpse of the private side of someone's public life.

The manuscript has travelled far and wide when in the making. It has taken shape in trains, 'planes and boats—on journeys stretching as far afield as Moscow and the Middle West of the United States. It has developed during quiet week-ends in the country; it has unravelled itself on a French cargo boat, when holidaying off the coast of North Africa. It has made staccato progress on non-pressurized aeroplanes over Eastern Europe, going to and from Moscow. At times it has made quite rapid progress on a 12,000-mile lecture tour of Canada and the United States, though it experienced neglect on the Observation Car of an American Zephyr train, with the surrounding country embraced by an awe-inspiring sunset. The neglect was heightened by the vision of a seemingly long silver cobra, winding its way ahead of the observation car—then the sudden intriguing realization that we ourselves were being towed by the silver cobra . . . abruptly the daylight faded, and under the glow of electric light the manuscript once more came into its own.

I am going to miss my companion of the last fifteen months' shared adventures, for a manuscript, I have discovered, is the ideal friend—silent and accommodating. It remains unresentful when mislaid, or when it is overworked by an attack of zeal and spare time on the part of the writer. It will stay submissive when erased, corrected and blue-pencilled to pieces. It exudes passive friendliness when you discard it after midnight, with a glow of content concerning your thoughts just expressed on its white surface. It turns the other cheek next morning, when, on re-reading your literary carryings-on of the night before, you are aghast: you forthwith erase rudely and scratch hysterically at the surface of your patient friend—and who knows if its passivity might not reflect the fact that it could have told you all this last night?

The manuscript is, above all, your kindest editor—for it does not condemn or argue: silently it shows you the insufferable depths of your grammatical errors—crashing clichés and befogged thinking.

I am going to miss exercising my mind with the vivid business of remembering things forgotten—delving backwards into time towards some incident glowing clearly, in a lost world that has made the correct year, day and date of the picture under survey of secondary importance. Such research spells tedium, and, as always, the amateur loses patience over matters that are concerned with dry precise reckoning.

Working over the last fifteen months, with the mental machine in full swing, I realize that I must always have wanted to have the companionship of a manuscript: for I recollect that there is one day in every week of my childhood that stands out with a persistent clarity of memory—I can still recall that it was on Wednesday that my governess demanded the writing of the schoolroom weekly essay. I also recollect that Tuesday was devoted to considerable anxiety on my part—for would she give me a subject next day that I would consider interesting? Would grown-ups never, never let me choose my own subjects?

•   •   •

During these present writings, something has emerged in the form of a sobering truth: I am convinced that we shape no event as forcibly as events shape us.

To pen an autobiography is to force to the front of your powers of observation the startling proof of your own lack of any real capacity to plan life. We are all aware of living life to the full on specific occasions—and with intense deliberation. If, though, these occasions are carefully scrutinized, it becomes clear that no carefully arranged basic plan brought them about: it is nearer the truth to admit that, at such times, we submit to the event, whose future shape and significance is unknown to us . . .

How many deep impressions we receive that bear no relation to the aims that we set out to achieve: the journey is taken for some particular objective, but it is not necessarily the fulfilment of the objective that stays with us through time—this is often quickly forgotten, and often changed by circumstances so as to be beyond recognition. What stays with us are sights, sounds, friendships, books, pictures; the meal eaten that owes its distinction to the surrounding landscape, or a curious turn of phrase in conversation; the memory of a new land seen at sunrise and at sunset remains with us when the life's purpose on that day has completely faded.

We carry within ourselves a curious medley of matter. We are unconscious hoarders: the range of the store is varied, the choice unrestrained, the result strangely intimate—unconcerned with our surroundings and their inhabitants. These inner realities cannot be shared with others, not even those dear to us. We hoard to nourish and sustain our individual solitude: that business of being alone, as we always must be, even in the largest of crowds. No one can elude his personal solitude (although he may waste it and ignore its importance). To elude it, however, would be to lose oneself, for to move away from the inner sense of reality is to develop a sickness—to become unaware of the meaning of one's individual entity in the whole.

Such experiences are perceived and understood quite differently by each one. Art and the artist succeed when they show us anew things that we know already; when they conjure up a vision that sows a seed to be reborn, in some other form, within ourselves.

It would seem that nothing belongs to any of us exclusively; everything is for all to see and interpret in a million different ways, and the sum total is life, in its infinite variety of individual living.

I

AN IRISH JIG

... 'What does it feel like to be old?' said the boy.

'It feels stiff like,' said the Philosopher.

'Is that all?' said the boy.

'I don't know,' the Philosopher replied after a few moments' silence. 'Can you tell me what it *looks* like to be young?'

'Why not?' said the boy, and then a slight look of perplexity crossed his face, and he continued, 'I don't think I can.'

'Young people,' said the Philosopher, 'do not know what age is, and old people forget what youth was. When you begin to grow old always think deeply of your youth, for an old man without memories is a wasted life, and nothing is worth remembering but our childhood. ...'

JAMES STEPHENS, *The Crock of Gold*

WHEN the adult mind would stir up childhood memories it sets itself a task, for it concerns itself with a time that contained the truth and significance of the passing moment, each hour of childhood being lived in full, and that is a rare event in later life. In the storeroom of a child's mind impressions wear clear bright colours, for they are imprinted on a virgin soil, a soil that is exceptionally receptive yet markedly selective. Very soon, however, the natural discernment of the young is replaced by ideas on growing up that are sown by adult minds; the new learning is mechanical and holds none of the wonderment of discovery. On such a day youth's first-born knowledge (in that small world once built up to live in apart) becomes as a dream and must go the way of outgrown toys. In the process of growing up a child soon ceases to be himself, for he is an atom that the world soon splits asunder.

When I was small I had a secret pastime; I would seek out one moment in the day when I would outflank (and with surprising skill) the watchful adult world and be alone. This process was known to me as 'a think'; it never went by any other name and was a very strictly disciplined recreation. I might resolutely fix my eyes on some near or distant object, a chair, a flower or a picture, and a story would be woven reaching from the birth to the death of the object. Sometimes I would decide on a personal transformation and I might choose to become a bird. That meant sitting under a tree and spotting the most suitable place to build my nest and there would follow great concentration, for the size and proportion of everything had to change; I became the exact size of a small bird and the tree as big as the surrounding country. If I took flight to another tree, I had left on a voyage; if I was lucky enough to find my two trees placed on each side of a brook, why there was the sea that I crossed in my flight; henceforth I was preoccupied with the joys and sorrows of myself in bird form.

I told no one of this pastime save my sister. She, with the inborn sense of a child's loyalty and understanding, left me respectfully un-molested; nor did she inform an adult of my flight into the world of imagery that even she was excluded from sharing.

But there was never very much time; I was acutely aware that my 'think' was limited, and round the corner was waiting that busy ordered world that I had managed to escape from for a brief magic moment.

•   •   •

Ireland in the first years of this century can only be portrayed if the reader will accept the youthful mind as I shall endeavour to recall it. A child has his own values, and his preoccupation with matters of trivial importance may play a part in the creating of an impression or the weaving of a pattern.

How can I record that time spent under the Wicklow Hills? Trivial indeed my pictures may seem to others, yet for me these pictures are intensely real; a great deal nearer to reality than much of my later life spent in the theatre.

I was born on 6 June 1898 and christened Edris (my family name is Stannus). My home, Baltiboys, a country house situated some two miles from the village of Blessington in County Wicklow, stood in the middle of a beautiful stretch of country at the foot of the Wick-low Hills. The original house was burnt in the rising of 1798; the house was now a long two-storied building with a spacious network of basement rooms. It was a typical Irish country house of about 1820–30, late Georgian in part, consisting of one main wing and two smaller ones.

As the firstborn of the family my elder sister was acclaimed by the ringing of the big yard bell and the lighting of a bonfire high up on the fox covert which could be seen for miles around. After her birth it was decided that all such festivities in the future should be curtailed, except in relation to the arrival of a son and heir. To the chagrin of all I was the next to enter the world, and so the bell did not ring and the prepared bonfire had to be hastily dismantled.

It was not until my ninth birthday that I heard the story and was deeply hurt. Later, when reprimanded for some misdeed, I announced that one day I might light my own bonfire.

My childhood, though, was quiet, and far removed from fulfilling ambitious dreams inspired by a sense of humiliation. I was intensely reserved and as obstinate as a mule—capable of 'the sulks' (as the nursery would say) brought to a fine art. If the situation, to my mind, warranted any extra stress, I was not above staging a hunger strike— noting with satisfaction the look of nervous apprehension in the adult eye: I was a delicate, undersized child, and this physical fact, I soon discovered, helped to heighten the dramatic impact of my action. I can only remember indulging in scrapes that risked no possi- bility of discovery, for to do anything that might result in detection and punishment struck me as a complete waste of time. My sister had quite a different philosophy; for her the game was always worth the candle, and consequently she was regarded as headstrong and her smaller sister as deceitful.

I have an early impression of an occasional savage contempt for adult reasoning and habits, and of controlling a surge of temper over correction or dictatorial reasoning. I can also recollect a fastidious reaction to grown-up speech and accents. At one time I suffered a nightly rage directed towards a kindly English nurse; to this harm- less being I had to say my prayers. The anger was caused because she would say 'Please Gawd'; I could not stand this mispronunciation, and there I knelt, hands together, eyes closed, longing to hit her; in despair one night I murmured: 'Oh God, get rid of her.'

As a nervous child, an accusation first frightened me, and as a reserved child it then humiliated me; finally my obstinacy developed a false pride, with the result that I went through an untruthful stage; oddly enough I can remember that this upset me in relation to myself, as much as it worried those in charge of me. But slowly temper would rise at the inquisitions of nurses and governesses; I lied, and without a prick of conscience; the reaction of a young mind that felt the indignity and humiliation of the whole proceedings.

My mind's eye can clearly see the curved Regency staircase leading to the upper story of the house. Next there comes to my memory the library, in which my grandmother read aloud to my sister and myself every evening after tea. I can still feel the excitement of winding my way down to the library to listen to my grandmother reading aloud the history of *The Swiss Family Robinson*, and my distress at the picture of the donkey caught in the coils of the snake. It was a very quiet room with books reaching from floor to ceiling; there were three long elegant windows, two looking on to the avenue and one on to the side of the house, from which could be seen the wooded grounds sloping down to the river Liffey, winding its way through the fields beyond the gardens.

I ask memory to take me up the staircase to the second floor of this rambling house. Built as three houses in one, there was a long passage that ran the length of the building; owing to the architectural structure of the house, this passage was broken by two small flights of stairs, one with four steps and one with only two. I can still feel myself running, and with an excited gasp hurling my body in the air to clear these stairs so as to continue the race at top speed.

Our schoolroom and nurseries were situated over the stables. They were low rooms, with windows small enough to be frowned on today, but the views were magnificent. One tiny window looked on to a courtyard, formed by the nursery part of the house, the stables, outbuildings and a high stone wall that had been built in the seventeenth century. This courtyard was entered through an arched gateway cut in the wall and the gateway was surmounted by a bell made of solid lead. The bell was always rung at midday, and it was the same bell which had remained silent when I entered the world.

Our courtyard was the occasional scene of a meet of the Kildare

Hunt. I can remember watching the meet from that small nursery window and later crossing the schoolroom to keep vigil at a window looking across the gardens; then away at the top of the fox hill one could see the hunt coming down the hillside in the sharp clear winter day, down towards the river still winding in the distance—and resembling in its wanderings a strip of metallic silver ribbon.

My memory now takes me indoors again and I return downstairs. When we reached the age of about five we were promoted to the dining-room for breakfast, and how cold this large room was in the winter! My father was often to be seen in a pink hunting coat, when an early breakfast would be eaten in a silence suggestive of speed and immediate action. The drawing-room seemed vast to me and we hardly ever entered it; it was the little morning-room that captured my imagination. Known as my mother's boudoir it opened on to the gardens through a french window and had delicate white furniture that my mother had decorated herself with coloured glass beads resembling giant-sized hundreds and thousands; it was a room full of light and family photographs and I loved it dearly.

Below stairs was the usual outlay of such country houses, for the kitchen world ran the entire length of the building. Endless white-washed rooms with stone flooring, in many places cold as a morgue. Kitchen, sculleries, pantry, still room, lamp room, meat room, laundry room, boot room, gun room, boiler room, servants' hall and servants' bedrooms. I see most clearly the lamp room, with its fantastic bulbous lamps of all shapes and sizes neatly arranged on shelves awaiting cleaning, trimming, and the polishing of intricate brass ornamentation. In those days, Irish country houses, even when they were situated a few miles from a well stocked village, had to be self-contained. Yet Baltiboys possessed only one bathroom, added at some earlier date, perhaps for fashion's sake. Tucked away in a corner in the main part of the house, it was fed by groaning pipes, and they in their turn were at the mercy of a temperamental boiler. In the hunting season, the children's bath-time was constantly in danger of interfering with the Captain's return from a day spent in the saddle. It was obvious that Paddy, the footman-valet, had his work cut out;

when very small we were flung into this huge bath like so many
sprats and occasionally we were aware of something resembling a
mild earthquake in the walls. This brought Paddy flying up from his
underground haunts; regardless of comfort or dignity a tap was
turned full blast on the sprats, and all was briefly summarized as 'the
water's boilin'.' Paddy, however, earned his Utopia, for he was later
to emigrate and become a butler in far-off New York where he was
to prosper surrounded by streamlined heating systems.

In the grounds we children lived long happy days. Though
deeply attached to many spots, my sister and I favoured in particular
the rookery. It was a large green slope on the extreme left of the
garden and had many great trees full of rooks, and a high deep
shrubbery shaped like a horseshoe. We played there for preference,
right through the four seasons of each year. It was here that the
solemn ritual of the burial of the dead robins took place; in the early
spring of the year we would bury these birds that could be found
frozen to death on lawn, paths and shrubbery. Japonica was plucked
from the house wall, three blossoms to each little grave. The mound
was shaped, and with the blossoms stuck in the earth, the result
resembled little red buttons in a neat row. A tear or two might be
shed for frozen robins in general, and then all was forgotten of the
long bitter winter.

From the front of the house a long avenue wound down to the
lodge at the gates; it had a park on one side and a wood of birch
trees on the other sloping down to the river bank. There was also a
walled kitchen garden, richly stocked. The wall was an old stone
one, rounded at the four corners and covered with fruit trees. I
always imagined that it was the most secret and sheltered spot in the
world, and as a child later in England, when I read *The Secret Garden*,
I visualized it as resembling the walled garden at Baltiboys. Beard,
the head gardener, always seemed to be at work here, either in the
greenhouses or bent double over the soil that produced a profusion
of perfect vegetables. We children were frightened of Beard; the
poor man was at times extremely tried by us and had more cause to
frown than to smile when we came in view.

I remember the awful day when my sister and I decided to strip a bed of hyacinths as an offering to a new governess from England, no doubt with the intention of winning her over to our side at the first instant. We were aware that a house party for the Punchestown Races was also due, but the importance of these guests in comparison to starting off on the right side of one of those English governesses seemed of no account. We were not aware of Beard though, charging down on us like an infuriated bull. He lost no time in dragging my poor father into the hubbub. We were both struck dumb rather more with surprise than remorse. My kind, wise father took everyone's side at once; he sympathized strongly with Beard and yet managed to convey to us that the roars still coming from his angry and painstaking gardener were tempered with a certain misunderstanding of our motives. It was enough for him to know that we had not picked the flowers for ourselves, or just to annoy Beard, and therefore were not being deliberately naughty. I stood by and watched his gentle understanding unfold; to this day I can recall how my heart bounded with relief at an example of that quietude that he always bestowed on us.

This affray, however, had its sequel a few nights later. I dreamt that the skies opened to reveal God. He proved to be Beard, not in a very good temper; he peeped at me through fluffy clouds, complete with bowler hat, walrus moustache and the usual patched corduroy trousers. But it did much to increase my awe of our gardener, for I never doubted the authenticity of my dream. I considered that I had had a revelation and that I should treat the whole matter with the secrecy that such a discovery deserved. As far as I was concerned all flower beds were left unmolested from that day.

Our daily walk very often took us across the fields to visit the home farm about a mile distant from the house. Here the herdsman, Finnigan, lived with his wife Kate; she was once my mother's nurse and later, when a widow, cook in our London home. Kate came into the family at nineteen and left it to die in retirement in her late seventies. She had two stepsons, John and Batch; the younger one was quite a hero in my eyes, for he would go down to the river and bring in the cows in the early evening. Once I was permitted to accompany him, leaving my governess and sister behind in the farm-house. I fell into the river and returned with my dress wet and muddy. The dress was removed, but my pinafore, which somehow had not come to grief, was put on again over my petticoat. I had bare arms and well can I remember my naked shame, crossing those wide fields, showing a pair of skinny arms and pursued by the scold-ings of an Edwardian governess, who did not hesitate to express her indignation that one of her charges had to walk abroad in such an improper state of clothing.

The farmhouse, with its great open hearth, had other memories for me. On arrival Kate would present us with large slices of newly baked soda bread smothered in rich home-churned butter. This 'tea' we were bidden to consume outside. I always hated my large slice and I can remember once burying it in the cabbage patch and wondering if it would give me away by growing up into a special sort of cabbage.

In that quiet country existence we were cut off from all communal interests and school life. Memory does not clarify why Kate singled me out and taught me how to execute an authentic Irish jig on the stone floor of that kitchen. If she had not done so, as this book will show, I might never have become a dancer. I adored my jig, for it was my first experience of any self expression.

Our lives were very sheltered: four small children with nurses and later nursery governesses. We had a steady flow of the latter, who all came from England and they did not stay very long. My sister and I regarded them almost as foreigners; strange, starched ladies with elegant mutton-sleeves, pork pie hats or boaters, and haughty Eng-lish accents—for one of their main tasks was to rectify our brogues. We found them either fussy or silly about country matters. One of them was assuredly the latter, for she wanted to see how the bull would react if she dressed herself in red. I can still see her as she stood on the gate wearing a red blouse and carrying a ridiculous red parasol which she waved excitedly at the bull. My sister and I stood in the rear filled with contempt tempered by a certain uneasiness. That day, however, the bull was as uninterested in red as he was in English governesses. We did not keep this story to ourselves and in no time the poor lady was on her way back to England.

Our Irish forms of transport in the first five years of this century belonged to another age. There was a curious affair called the steam tram, just a tram with a long funnelled engine drawing it. This ran through Blessington village to Dublin, a distance of twenty miles, but the journey took one and a half hours or longer. The lines ran by the side of the country road unlit by any form of lamps. All along the line at intervals there were to be found little white stone crosses; thus were marked the spots where inebriated Irishmen lay down to sleep on the rails after fairs or wakes and were not spotted by the tram driver. Cows also had a way of blocking progress by resting on the lines and causing the tram to be late.

Our own domestic transport was complicated. Today a service-able family car would suffice, but not so in those days. The most prominent vehicle in our nursery lives was the governess cart, a low rotund little carriage drawn by donkey or small pony, the whole haphazardly controlled by the governess. We just rolled about inside, but in easy reach of the restraining hand of the nurse. The torture of the winter drives is still fresh in my mind. Unless held up by really heavy snow we made one pilgrimage a day into Blessington in the early afternoon to fetch the English mail; I now strongly suspect that our homesick English governesses volunteered to do this, rather than trust to the groom finding time to ride in. I have vivid recollections of whimpering over the pain of my frozen hands and feet as I stag-gered up the stairs and down the long passage; there was only one thought in my mind and that was to seek out the nursery fire.

On Sundays, we were elevated to the Irish sidecar. Accompanied by grown-ups, who clutched us almost as firmly as we clutched our Sunday hats, we would be driven in to church by the groom. In church we were shut up in one of three family pews suspended at the back over the heads of the ordinary church pews. It was a square box-like affair with a little door into it, and my head just appeared over the top. My dearest ambition was to sit in one of the long pews

down below, for these pews appeared to me to hold a great number
of exciting people.

My father had a dogcart, and there was also a brake and a
brougham. I dreaded the brougham, for once I sank into its gloomy
depths, which smelt of harness polish and cracked old leather, I was
promptly sick. It held the further menace of being the form of
winter transport to children's parties in other country houses and it
was customary to drive several miles to these affairs. I was intensely
shy and suffered tortures. Wisely, no one took any notice; I went,
was sick, cried and came home again, while my sister was in a constant frenzy of delight, and her pleasure made me feel more out of
things than ever. The brake conjures up house parties setting off for
race meetings, and the family luggage embarking on the yearly pilgrimage to Folkestone for one month in the summer. Punchestown
Races and the spring were just one and the same thing. Visitors filled
the house; I can remember standing on the steps with my sister
watching them pile into the brake, the women with their bonnets
and hats tied on with flowing veils.

One of our other forms of daily exercise consisted of bowling our
hoops in the grounds and we must have covered miles racing up and
down paths. We were often tempted to stop and hunt for birds'
nests, a pastime strictly forbidden. I can see one beautiful little nest
full of eggs: fascinated by the beauty of the small eggs, I picked one
up, but its delicate shell broke and stained the hem of my pinafore.
Back in the schoolroom, standing in front of my governess saying
my tables, I saw her eyes travel to the tell-tale stain. We were both
informed that little girls who killed little birds would probably have
their eyes pecked out by the mother bird. My sister was unmoved,
for she was two years my senior and anyway far more adventurous
and courageous. I felt that this particular form of an eye for an eye
was terrible but not unreasonable; it struck my imagination that the
death of the bird could be expected to end in the death of my eyes.
Thus there were no tears or loud protests when, having wholly forgotten their prophecy, unthinking nursery guardians ordered me
once more into the garden for exercise. I obeyed, sick at heart and

faint with fear; for about three days I managed to bowl my hoop along those well-known paths with my eyes tight shut, opening them for a second when driven to do so. At the end of that time I pondered on the possibility of grown-up fallibility or the shortness of a mother-bird's memory; suddenly my sin became a thing of the past and fear faded away.

The mind of the child holds on to specific highlights, and certain world events stand out clearly through some link with the intimate life of the home. For me, one of the most vivid is the Russo-Japanese war, and I recall a conversation on this matter between my grandmother and father in the sidecar when returning from church. The news from Russia had been grave and I was puzzled, for Russia conjured up a picture of a strange race vaguely known as Cossacks, and I thought of them as fierce giants with enormous beards. The Jap I imagined to be about the size of a Leprechaun. I saw it all as a war of giants and pygmies, and I felt that my prayers must be for the pygmies.

●　　　●　　　●

I find myself on the top of the fox hill, clinging to the hand of my nurse. There is a huge bonfire erected; it seems to me to reach up into the skies and to bear the shape of a wigwam. I do not know what time of day it was, but I fancy that it must have been very early evening. I can remember crouching on the grass to see, underneath, a tiny glow of fire. Around me it was said that the Captain was returning, and his return seemed to have some connection with a faraway calamity called the Boer War. I am next sitting up in bed in the nursery, the door opens and a soldier comes in wearing a forage cap. It is my father. That is all that I know of that long passage of time since he sailed away with his regiment, was wounded and made prisoner, and returned to Ireland to be greeted by the glow of a bonfire, his two astonished little daughters, and the son who had been born in his absence.

The landscape is illuminated by remembered visits to cottagers living on the estate. Some of the old women were like witches, and many a story did my imagination weave around them in such a guise. We would bring them small gifts, and stand by in awe as our governess made conversation with the owners of these deeply furrowed faces; a knotted hand might be holding the clay pipe, while their bare feet rested on the hearth and their faces were sharply outlined by the large black shawls covering their heads and most of their bodies. Small animals from the farmyard came and went—in and out of these kitchens at will. Upon our exit these old women's strange blessings would follow us down the muddy little front paths. Other cottages might swarm with children reared on a diet of potatoes, porridge and an occasional piece of bacon. The acceptance of poverty had a more nonchalant than stoic quality about it and there was a great deal of tuberculosis; these peasants had large families and there was the superstition that the seventh son in any family had the power of 'the cure' or what we call the gift of healing.

It is the Irish tinkers that stand out as the most frightening of human spectacles; they resembled Romany gipsies disguised as bedraggled ravens and could be guaranteed to frighten any child; I may add that this attitude of fear was encouraged by the constant threats of Irish nurses that naughtiness might end in the tinkers getting you one day. I also dreaded a 'wake', or rather the promoters returning from one; once I witnessed a coffin rolling off a cart into the ditch, and that macabre accident was due to the state of those in charge of the burial after the 'wake'.

One must allow for the passage of time and the vivid exaggeration that fear can implant in the mind of a child. Fear concerning drunkards is with me, though, to this day, and Blessington Fair is partly responsible for my reaction. Fifty years ago it was a morbid source of entertainment to those in charge of us—for what to me was a hideous spectacle, both nurse and governess appeared to enjoy. Our village had four public houses and on fair days trade was very brisk. We were driven in to witness the fun; seated in the small governess cart I became acutely aware that the vehicle was small and defenceless, and I would sit frozen with panic at the drunken fights. Once I saw a child flung into the air as one might toss a football and that reduced me to shrieks as loud as any of those surrounding me. Even when driving home through the lanes it always took time to rid ourselves of the fair; we would have to pass reeling argumentative tinkers, stray carts partly overturned in ditches, tramps and peasant farmers straggling across the road.

We travelled but little: only to make the annual pilgrimage to Folkestone and the occasional ceremonial visit to my paternal grandfather who lived in Portarlington. By the constant selling of land my grandfather managed to live on a dwindling income. He met the changing times quietly, without any attempt at a solution. There had to be the daily carriage drive that he could ill afford; it was made possible by disguising the gardener as groom. Half the old family livery—the upper half—was intact, but the trousers were missing, for they had fallen to pieces and new ones represented a great extravagance. So the gardener wore his gardening trousers; he was placed on the box heavily encased in a large rug and forbidden to move under any circumstances. I remember little of my grandfather beyond kind humorous eyes, gentle grumblings and genteel carriage drives.

•   •   •

Did I ever, during those seven formative years, get a glimpse of the life that was to be mine in the years to come? Perhaps I had two small symbolic moments. The clear-cut joy of my first theatre visit— this was to the Gaiety Theatre in Dublin. Prophetically it was the pantomime of *The Sleeping Beauty*. I can see the enraged Carabosse in the form of a witch with demon king attendant, setting off in a sleigh that seemed to fly across the stage, filling me with an anxiety as to its progress when out of sight. I can further conjure up the Princess on her birthday. The stage was a great garden of outsized roses and she a slim girl with a Rossetti-like face and hair; I can see her so clearly, in a curious pre-Raphaelite tawny-coloured gown as she ran down the stage exclaiming on the beauty of the day. With that vision everything fades, except that I remember her as most wondrously beautiful.

The other was a more curious experience. I have already recorded the fact that in that remote country place I was taught my first dance, an Irish jig, and I have spoken of my misery at children's parties. I was attending one party and as usual spent the time clinging to my nurse's skirts. To distract me, my mother stood me on a chair to witness a dance by a Miss Leggatt Byrne (I think that she was either the daughter or niece of the well-known teacher of that name in Dublin). Something within me underwent a complete change. I forgot the awful party and the crowd of people; a curious critical faculty suddenly arose within me and I found myself consumed with interest, but not overcome with admiration. She wore a wide accordion-pleated dress edged with lace and my mother informed me that she was executing a skirt dance. I did not feel like the little girl who had watched the pantomime, where all had aroused sheer un-critical delight: in this case I watched something that aroused my deepest interest, but without any of the whole-hearted pleasure that it was bestowing on my mother and others. Suddenly I found that my interest had wholly switched to the lady at the piano, for I saw that she watched the dancer very closely. I was charged with a fierce longing; I desperately wanted her to play for my own precious dance, for I knew the tune as Kate had often hummed it to me. I decided that mine was by far the better dance, in fact I found this one silly by comparison. I then electrified my mother by saying that I would like to do my Irish jig if the lady at the piano would play the tune.

I experienced no fears; I had no thought for the people surrounding me when I stood in the middle of the room waiting to start, though I had a real anxiety that the conversation at the piano might not result in the lady understanding about the tune. I can remember very distinctly hoping—as a fully-fledged professional might—that she would get things right and that she would understand what I wanted. Of course, when it was over, I was as before, hiding behind my nurse and refusing to plunge my hand in the dreaded bran pie.

•   •   •

THE AUTHOR'S
MOTHER WITH
THELMA (1900)

THE AUTHOR'S
MOTHER WITH
HER FOUR
CHILDREN—
THELMA, EDRIS,
TREVOR AND
GORDON (1904)

THE AUTHOR'S
GRANDMOTHER
(1900)

THE AUTHOR'S
FATHER (1916)

As a ripple on a quiet stream, we children began to realize that life was preparing a big change for us. Our parents and grandmother spoke more often of England; we began to hear something of the needs of big houses, and the necessity of only rich people living in them. Servants threw out hints, the younger ones spoke of emigration and the older ones were seen to weep.

A day arrived one very early spring when the last trunks were strapped and we were bidden to say our special good-byes. We were taken down the avenue to visit Mrs. Roberts, the lodge keeper's wife; she followed us as we returned to the house, crying as if her heart would break and raising her white apron to cover her face; for her grief was pagan in its stark simplicity and too immense for the duties of a pocket handkerchief.

I have one more clear-cut vision to recall of that strange day. I can recall it with all its undiminished and astonished sadness, for children can be astonished to find themselves sad. Change, with all its confusing upheaval, is thrust on them and in such events they play no particular part.

I was left standing midst the bustle of departure, at the window of our old nursery. My eyes looked on the lawns and paths of those gardens that I would play in no more. On that early gentle day in spring the sun was already making long shadows. A gardener was cutting a long strip of turf near the top of the centre lawn; slowly and quietly it was rolled. I watched, weighed down with an unhappiness that I could not analyse; I found myself thinking that the turf resembled nothing more than a gigantic green Swiss roll. I knew suddenly that never again, when such things happened to change the visual outlook of the gardens, would I be able to await the why and wherefore of it all, for the great sea was to come between us and the end of the Swiss roll would be someone else's concern.

I did not cry, nor did I ask any questions as to when we might be coming back; I knew the truth and I wanted no comforting grown-up lies. There and then I deliberately tore my heart out and left it, as it were, on the nursery window-sill. I remember nothing of the journey, for Ireland had faded—Ireland with its sights and sounds, its soft air and smell of burning peat. Yet there has always been the secret fantasy picture of a gigantic green Swiss roll, whose ultimate fate was never known to me.

It is thus that impressions become woven into the life pattern. They cause us to remember the thoughts of Ireland's great poet:

"*I have spread my dreams under your feet*
Tread softly because you tread on my dreams."

II

THE LONGEST WAY

'There isn't a drop of Balzac blood in him, I said to myself; he is pure Turgenev, and perhaps Ireland is a little Russia in which the longest way round is always the shortest way home and the means more important than the end. . . .'

GEORGE MOORE, *Hail and Farewell*

CHILDHOOD in England began for me within twenty-four hours of my parting with the green Swiss roll. It commenced in an atmosphere of late Victorian peace and order, for our grandmother took us to live with her at the seaside; our home was to be in Walmer—a small seaside town adjoining Deal.

Within a few months everything changed. The rowdy, sinister tinkers of the Blessington Fair were replaced by happy, well-clothed human beings, scornfully alluded to as trippers. They invaded the Deal end in the summer, and were considered to be a great annoyance to the residents. They appeared to do all those things that my grand-mother regarded as vulgar, but I decided that such pastimes made life worth living in this strange and formal England. I longed to grow up and become a tripper in my own right; to go out to sea in a small boat with a concertina and buns in a bag; to bathe with a crowd of people in the middle of the day, and not before breakfast because the beach was empty; to pay twopence and go to all the pierrot shows on the beach; to ride donkeys; to listen to the band in the evenings instead of going to bed; to live in those mysterious small houses, with bow windows sticking out over the pavements and cards in the windows on which was written 'Apartments'; to par-take of a tripper tea which always seemed to include things called shrimps. During my first lonely summer of adaptation to a changed order of living my lively trippers appeared carefree, noisy and happy, just as I was (momentarily) carefilled, quiet and unhappy.

My grandmother's house (small as it seemed after Baltiboys) with its quarter acre of garden looking on to the sea front, nevertheless had its own individuality. A house of the late 'seventies, it had the period comfort to make up for its lack of any architectural interest.

My grandmother had inherited it from a kinsman. He had been a distinguished general and the house, with his medals, was a monument to his memory and his fierce campaigns. A large, splayed tiger with a well-stuffed head, open mouth and outsize glass eyes greeted you when you entered the hall. On its flattened back it supported a giant green porcelain pedestal jar that held a huge aspidistra. The General had shot the tiger in India at a moment not concerned with other more important shootings. My grandmother tended the aspidistra, washing the long green leaves with a soapy sponge. Sometimes I wondered which had lived in that part of the hall the longer—the tiger or the aspidistra.

Up the front stairway were hung engravings of the General's battles: fierce pictures depicting white and black soldiers in head-on clashes of sword and spear. English soldiers with beards, moustaches and sun helmets were depicted in noble last stands, sometimes kneeling four-square, with fire spitting from their rifles in defiance of hundreds of natives, who leapt down the hillside with daggers between their teeth. Over the more important pictures were draped the battle relics, tattered blood-stained flags captured or carried by the General and his campaigners.

It did not take long for Beard, our old head gardener in far-off Ireland, to lose his status as God in my small life. I was a little older now and was the victim of a different and more cheerful form of awe: hero-worship of the General; but Trevor, the elder of my two brothers—never quite forgiven by me for confiscating the bonfire—intervened once more, for he could boast that the General was his godfather.

Here, too, there was a library; to this sanctuary I took myself along with my sore heart and puzzled head. It was a high, small room, and the one big window looked on to a little shrubbery. Here in the library the General still followed me. He hung on the wall in the form of a large photograph, and looked down with fierce penetrating eyes. His breast was covered with those medals bestowed on him as mark of his country's esteem for settling the events that had inspired the pictures on the stairs. He was an exceedingly handsome old gentleman with his snow-white hair, side whiskers and moustaches—an English version of Bismarck. My eyes would wander down the wall to a table topped with a glass case. Here the General appeared to break up into several colourful exhibitions. Open to my gaze was each medal in its case, his sword, his insignia of knighthood and his miniature. When I sank into a chair to read I sank into the General's rocking-chair; my small legs at first could not reach the floor, so I rocked incessantly as I read.

How I read! I think that I acquired, by the age of ten, quite an astonishing survey of Victoria's reign through nothing less than the magnificently bound copies of *Punch* dating from the first number up to the beginning of King Edward's reign. I can still remember staggering across the library to the rocking-chair clutching a volume almost as heavy as myself. Through the changing fashions lavishly illustrated, the political and the war cartoons, the jokes, much of the editorial matter, and in the later volumes the series of Du Maurier drawings, almost the entire nineteenth century in England took form under my eyes, leaving a kaleidoscopic impression more enlightening to my child's mind than the schoolroom history book. Other works on the bookshelves I can still feel myself handling; a richly bound series called *Masterpieces of the World's Literature*, *The Keepsake*, Shakespearean works fully illustrated, Scott, Dickens and the lilac, green and yellow fairy books. Filling a low, revolving bookcase was an edition in some very large volumes of Byron's complete works. My hero-worship underwent another change; the Byron portraits represented my idea of male perfection and I would not let myself think about his lameness. I read *Childe Harold* when very young and it made a deep impression on me.

Those hours spent in the library were encouraged by my grandmother, who cherished hopes that I would grow up 'clever' . . . I faintly sensed this hope on the part of other grown-ups; I suspect that it was based on the fact that I was plain and inconspicuous next to my very beautiful sister. I can remember standing in front of a mirror and beseeching God to make me beautiful, and suggesting that if He would do so I would not bother Him about making me good as well.

I longed for a beautiful face, and chose all my little friends from the prettier specimens. An elderly couple, friends of my grandmother, told her that they had noted the pretty legs and feet of her youngest granddaughter. My grandmother, who was convinced that I needed 'encouragement', decided to tell me what had been said to her. How quickly I ran upstairs to my bedroom so as to climb on a chair and tilt the small dressing-table mirror: the serviceable serge skirt was pulled up: I gazed at thin legs encased in brown cashmere stockings and small feet shod in strong laced shoes. I reflected that this was the result of my fervent prayers; no matter if the beautifying process was starting at the wrong end.

When I had reached the age of about 13 my grandmother had a rude awakening as to the wisdom of allowing me the run of the General's supposedly unblemished library. High up on the top shelf I had discovered a book, a translation from the French. When it was noted that I was reading a French book, my governess was asked to glance at it. From that day onwards all top shelf readings were out of bounds, for the book turned out to be Gautier's *Mademoiselle de Maupin*.

Like all children of seven I soon adapted myself to this new life in England, and a very happy and contented one it became. Parties I now enjoyed as much as my sister enjoyed them. I went to a weekly dancing class clutching a skipping-rope and a pair of clubs. I can still feel the intense excitement of this Monday afternoon treat; I went with my sister and governess in a hired brougham to a girls' school in Upper Deal. We wore party frocks and white lambs' wool 'Red Riding Hood' capes lined with pale blue silk. Our hands were covered in fine lace mittens and our legs encased in long open-work black stockings. Later in the week we visited the same school again; but for me this latter outing was terrifying. It was gym, and gym under a sergeant-major of the Marines. He looked like the Kaiser and treated us as small soldiers. Muffled in a huge, white sweater,

with a rolled collar into which I had considerable difficulty in keeping my nose from disappearing, I was the smallest and quite the most
ridiculous spectacle in the class. I hated that man, for he treated me
with a kindly indifference that made me dislike him more every
week. The culmination arrived when he seized me playfully by the
back of the neck of my sweater and the seat of my dark blue serge
bloomers and hoisted me over the 'horse', that I was much too tiny
to clear on my own. I was humiliated and furious beyond words,
and deeply resented the amusement of my grandmother and
governess.

We lived this well-ordered life for about three years, from my
eighth to my eleventh year. Towards the middle period I imposed
tasks on myself that took up all my spare time. I decided that I must
edit a small magazine of short stories for the benefit of my sister and
two brothers. I spent much energy writing the stories and more on
making my sister and elder brother read them. I developed a passion
for something that I had only been to once in my life—the theatre.
Every Sunday my nursery companions had to sit through a play
written by me. I cut figures out of magazines and put string through
the top of their heads and stuck them on cardboard. The nursery
window-sill was the stage and the blind came down over it with the
smack of an efficient curtain. The plays proved to be far more popular than my magazine. Restless dreams and a tendency to sleep-walk
curtailed these activities; the family doctor had a lot to say about an
over-active brain.

•   •   •

The pattern of my future was gradually shaping. The dancing
teacher, who came from London every week, was the head assistant
of the well-known amateur teacher, Mrs. Wordsworth. She spoke of
my talent to my grandmother, who had noted how often I begged
her to play for me to dance.

In my grandmother's Victorian drawing-room I would ask, of a
winter evening, to push back the heavily fringed and antimacassared

chairs . . . this would leave a small clear space on the thick Oriental carpet. There was no light save the fire and the flickering candles in their brass stands on the upright piano; the floral design of inlaid wood on the panel above the keyboard is still a distinct picture. My grandmother sat very upright in her evening gown of stiff black moiré silk—the bodice crossed over with a delicate lace fichu held in place by a large cameo brooch. Her grey hair would be surmounted by an evening cap of lace adorned with a black velvet bow. Resolutely she would accompany me, concentrating on the music with the aid of her pince-nez attached to its long slender gold chain.

The rest of the room was in shadow; there were the cabinets of 'foreign' china collected by the General, faintly shaking behind the glass cases, and on the walls a collection of pale aquatints of dead relations. I danced earnestly, with only the fireplace as my audience, and as I danced I wove strange stories around my improvisations.

Then it would be bedtime and my grandmother, folding up the music, would bid me return to the nurseries. Running up to that childhood world under the roof I would experience a strange sense of happy achievement; it was an ecstasy that lifted me beyond the petty irritation of nursery discipline at close of day: I would go contentedly to bed, wrapped in my new-found secret happiness.

My grandmother decided to pass on my dancing teacher's opinion of my talent to my mother in London and she, in her turn, remembered the episode of the Irish jig. Suddenly my mother appeared and took me away for a two-day visit to London; I was brought to the Empire to see Adeline Genée dance.

In Ireland I was introduced to the theatre by the pantomime of *The Sleeping Beauty*; in England I was introduced to the ballet by a production called *The Belle of the Ball*. On the stage were the great Genée and a little English girl called Phyllis Bedells, and on the back-cloth was a painting of the glass domed market next to the Royal Opera House. Today, I look on this dome from my office window. . . .

By my eleventh birthday we were installed in a large London flat in Harrington Road with my mother, and only the summer was spent in Walmer.

The schoolroom now held three of us. Our education was stimulated by the bestowal of qualifying labels called 'stars' and 'stripes'. ... My 'stars' had the same monotony about them as my 'stripes'. The former were always received for composition and drawing, the latter for untidiness, dawdling and arguing. Occasionally the stripe would descend on me in the form of a 'double'—and that doubtful reward was for Arguing About Religion. My mother had to sit at the head of the table, on Saturday mornings, to hear the virtues and vices of three of her offspring (ranging from six to twelve years of age) read aloud—for it was all tied up, in a sinister fashion, with our pocket money. One morning my precocious small self espied the fact that she was trying very hard not to laugh. ... During the spring of my eleventh year, I nearly died of nothing more romantic than measles: my small brothers had been hastily returned to my grandmother, and my father came over from Ireland. How indignant I was, during convalescence, once more to hear a funny story at my expense. My brother, Trevor, had been told by his grandmother that he could not go to some local school sports 'as his sister was dangerously ill'. On the receipt at Walmer of the news that the crisis was past—his only comment was: 'Now we can go to the sports.'

My dancing continued at Mrs. Wordsworth's School where I went four times every week. I had only one other interest, I suppose something left over from my country-bred childhood: this was a real love of horses. My mother drove a great deal; she would sometimes drive at Olympia for Smith, the big horse dealer, whose London stables were close to our London flat. She would take me down there and I made friends with the head groom. He would sometimes take me with him, before breakfast, into the Park in a dogcart; I have happy memories of learning to drive under his guidance, and I often drove round Rotten Row, deserted as it was at that early hour of the morning.

We next moved from the flat to a five-story house in Earls Court

Square. Mrs. Wordsworth's was my one interest now, and I can still see that Edwardian School of Deportment.

·   ·   ·

It is a ballroom—the Queensberry Hall, Harrington Road. Some sixty little girls are ranged in the centre of the highly polished floor. Around the large oval-shaped hall is placed an unbroken single line of upright gilt chairs. These are occupied by nannies, governesses, and a representative gathering of mothers—*Debrett* and otherwise. To the strains of a large grand piano, a dignified head teacher is keeping the dancing class on the move. The little girls are mainly attired in accordion-pleated dresses of various colours, long black silk stockings, and the inevitable mittens; lace or ruching edged the pleated dresses—dresses inspired by Loie Fuller who was all the rage. There is also a smattering of silk party dresses with big sashes and long sleeves.

At the far end of the hall the office door opens and in sweeps a plump, dumpy old lady. What an entrance!—the long black silk dress ending in a train, lace at the throat, tiny plump hands encased in short white kid gloves are crossed over the stomach, and a lace handkerchief dangles from two fingers. The figure is erect, imposing, possibly modelled on Queen Victoria; it resembles a neat little yacht in full sail. 'Dance it, children . . . dance it'—and the voice is a siren rising above the music. Rows of small heads are held higher and skirts are played with greater zeal, and the gathering of mothers would noticeably straighten their backs and uncross their feet.

Mrs. Wordsworth has reached the top of the class and the music stops. Some of us may be seized from the third or fourth row and brought to the front. If this is to be our fate we must give the black figure our full attention, for 'Come here' is the booming command; but one eye is a very glassy glass eye that by no chance ever looks at the child that the voice is addressing. We may receive that exciting command: 'Sit down, children, backs up.' Down we go like obliging little Buddhas.

If there was a sweeping circular promenade embracing all gilt chairs it meant that the mothers were for it, to everyone's delight, including the mothers. A long pause . . . 'How can a mere child grow into an elegant young woman, worthy of her court curtsey, if the mother sits in a heap with her feet crossed?' . . . the glass eye does its work, but it is to be noted that the owner never wastes its glassy stare on the untitled. Again, another day: 'By chance I have just heard an argument between mother and child as to how to wear the school satchel. The child wished to wear it hanging in front, the mother on one side—as prescribed by some foolish headmistress. [Pause] The child was right, the mother was wrong. How can a silly parent expect a child to grow up straight wearing something resembling a soldier's knapsack that drags the child's shoulder down from the tender age of eight? Mothers, visit your schools and do something about something for once.' Another pause, followed by a booming: 'Now, children—all together—dance it, children, dance it.' We scramble to our feet and chassé with renewed zeal.

Mrs. Wordsworth's class answered to a system that was known as Fancy Dancing; a quaint compromise of rudimentary steps such as the chassé and glissade combined with other steps fancy beyond belief. We were, however, none the worse for it; it was harmless and good fun. It was also singularly fortunate that any attempt to stand on the toes was frowned upon, not on account of any regard for the welfare of our feet, but because it was considered theatrical, and Mrs. Wordsworth had a puritanical loathing of dancing as a profession. She regarded it the duty of anyone under her tuition to eschew the theatrical profession at all costs. I wasted valuable years as a Wordsworth show pupil displaying a pair of painfully untheatrical feet.

But during this Wordsworth period I was taken to see all the great dancers. The Russians at both Covent Garden and the Coliseum and Pavlova at the Palace on her special Wednesday matinées. I had a little friend at Mrs. Wordsworth's who was one of Pavlova's eight special child pupils, and my envy and misery knew no bounds. Her father was a member of the editorial staff of one of the daily newspapers, and consequently could obtain the necessary introduction. I stood little chance with my miserable background of tinkers and generals—and well I knew it.

My mother, however, realized that the situation must end; she had concluded that I must have some talent and should be properly trained. There was a stormy scene with the old lady, who was bent on my becoming a pupil teacher. She informed my mother that she would scrub floors before a daughter of hers went near the stage; but my mother grimly assured her that she would have me trained so as to avoid my having to scrub floors for myself.

That ended my days with Mrs. Wordsworth and her vast money-making concern. She never asked to see me again, nor did she inquire after my progress. I was, according to her lights, a prodigal that could not return.

I last heard of her from my two brothers, who, as schoolboys, one holiday were on a farm that adjoined the old lady's property. They were permitted to row a boat on her lake. One day, when they were in some difficulty, a certain dumpy figure—this time in a serviceable black coat and skirt—was to be seen on the shore . . . 'Come on, row, you silly boys, row!' boomed across the lake . . .

If I had been there it would surely have sounded like 'Dance, you silly child, dance. . . .'

•   •   •

The break with Mrs. Wordsworth led to the first big change in my life; I was, at last, to be trained as a professional dancer. This must have happened round about my twelfth to thirteenth year—quite late by the standards of today. I was sent to the Lila Field Academy for Children, a theatre school run by two sisters who were German by origin. Here I executed my first barre exercises under a picture of a group of children in a play entitled *The Goldfish*.

There was a boy in the picture, a jester. He had just left the school and had his feet on the lower rungs of the theatre ladder. I was told how clever he was; I asked his name and was informed that he was called Noel Coward. So I executed my exercises with a sigh and my eyes on 'Noel' who was so much ahead of me as to be already in the theatre and accepted as clever. Was I, I wondered, ever going to catch up and be noticed by anyone? The theatre boasted of child dancing stars in those days. Phyllis Bedells whom I had once seen at the Empire, and now there were even younger ones such as Mavis Yorke and Elise Craven; then there was this Noel Coward who came from my own school and was going to be a great actor. I began to feel that my parents had been too long making up their minds.

The Lila Field Academy was a typical theatrical school. We learnt something of everything, but I was almost immediately set aside to specialize in the classical ballet section. Early in 1913 I went on tour with a Company consisting of children from the school. I was four-teen and a half. We were called The Wonder Children and presented an astonishing and rather terrible programme of small ballets and short plays. I can also remember a precocious effort in the form of a revue—with the children depicting great stars. Needless to say I was doomed to be Pavlova and executed The Dying Swan, having laboriously noted this down myself from the upper circle of the Palace Theatre. I had two cousins acting in the cast, and as their mother was with them it was arranged that I should be under her care. All the children had either a mother or grown-up sister with them.

I think that I can boast of having danced on every old pier theatre in England! We worked very hard; I made ten solo appearances every night and received a salary of £4 per week. Out of this I kept myself, paid my term's tuition fees and saved. Lodging in full in those days cost about £1 per week. I can recall one very good board-ing house at Eastbourne taking us all for 17/- per week inclusive.

We had no wardrobe mistress and no dressers. My mother had to buy my ten costumes and I had to take them with me in my own theatre hamper. I was responsible for packing and unpacking, mending, ironing, and all necessary laundry work of these costumes and the care of my shoes and tights; this was coupled with eight performances per week and long Sunday journeys. I also had to assist my cousin in writing for rooms to different addresses as I was older (by two years) than her two daughters. Miss Field was very strict, and our clothes and make-up had to be exactly as she ordained. The discipline was good, and we had her sister always in charge and an excellent manager, Val Kimm by name, who always 'took out' *Peter Pan*. The tours were short, and in between them, when back in London, I returned to the schoolroom and my governess. I was very careful of money because I knew that I must save if I was to continue my training, as my mother could not shoulder the full responsibility. My only extravagance was books; about every second week on tour I bought a classic in a certain Collins series at 2s. a volume. For poetry, my great love, I would pay more, as I longed to have all my poetry between limp morocco leather covers and the leaves gilt edged. I remember my conscience troubling me one day when I walked back to our lodgings with such a copy of Tennyson, for which I had paid 6s. My cousin scolded me, for she considered that I required new stockings. However, although I took great pride in my theatre clothes I had no interest at all in my everyday appearance. It was no good scolding me; I wanted one day to have my own library, because of the happy hours that a library had already given me . . .

My mother, very naturally, disapproved of these tours; she was worried about my education, my ragamuffin outlook on many things, and my independence. When I returned to London she would send me to auditions in the hope that I could get something to do in London. I hated those ordeals and felt nervous and inferior. I never succeeded in getting anything; I was either not what they wanted or I arrived after someone else had obtained the engagement. Only once did I enjoy an audition, although it appeared that I was again too late; but the kindly Sir Charles Hawtrey said he would see me dance

THE OLD BRIDGE LEADING TO BALTIBOYS IN THE NINETEENTH
CENTURY

BALTIBOYS FROM THE AIR (1955)

BALTIBOYS YARD BELL

after his matinée. I had no fear that day and must have shown the fact, for he asked me to dance three different dances. Afterwards he came round and talked to me. He said that he had nothing for me in *Where the Rainbow Ends* but if anyone ever tried to discourage me I was to promise him that I would not take any notice. I went home jobless but treading on air.

When I look back on those wasted years between ten and fifteen I only feel a renewed anxiety to leave English dancers with some security and definite standards. Coming from an untheatrical background it was impossible for my mother to understand what I really needed and to know whom to turn to for advice. In those days England had no Sadler's Wells, no Arts Council, no big private schools, and no institution such as the Royal Academy of Dancing devoting its work to raising the standard of teaching and giving advice and guidance throughout the country. The ballet was not recognized as a branch of the English Theatre; dancers were accepted as individuals on their individual merits and they had to search for their own teachers; how they arrived at their eventual state of execution was no one's concern.

•   •   •

It is the summer of 1914 and I am sixteen; we are on tour again, visiting seaside towns. The town is Southsea and it is the first week of August; vivid indeed is the memory of that performance on the South Parade Pier on the eve of 4th August. The house was packed, not only with my once loved trippers, but with tension . . . a girl in the Company is in tears, for her brother—a naval officer on leave—has had to rejoin his ship that evening.

Next day we are at war and within two weeks the Company is disbanded for good at Leamington.

I spent the rest of that terrible summer at Walmer within sound of the heavy gunfire in France and with the news growing ever more grave.

It was the end of an epoch: many of us were to grow up suddenly

4

and with the memory of Sir Edward Grey's grim statement: 'The lamps are going out all over Europe; we shall not see them lit again in our lifetime. . . .'

•   •   •

On a cold morning in the very late autumn of 1914 several children and young girls stood in the wings of the Lyceum Theatre with numbers pinned on the front of their dresses—it was an audition for the Christmas pantomime. No. 6 was very nervous and her feet were terribly cold. Somewhere back in the dark red and gold theatre sat the Brothers Melville; rich but shabby, they appeared to resemble those comics 'The Brokers'—traditional pantomime characters. With them was little Madame Rosa, the ballet mistress, and Sullivan the conductor, known throughout the theatre as 'The Nephew of Sir Arthur'. Everyone danced and No. 6 felt, despite her nerves and her cold feet, that she had not done herself an injustice when on the huge stage. She was right; while she was waiting at the side with the others when it was all over, the Nephew of Sir Arthur suddenly came through the pass door on his way out of the theatre; some spirit of compassion for all those young but anxious face must have seized him . . . for he paused by No. 6 and whispered briefly: 'You've won . . .'

Winning meant that I had got my first London engagement as principal dancer in the Lyceum pantomime, the pantomime that was to play through the first winter of World War I in London. This engagement resulted in an annual appearance for me in this theatre until the winter of 1919.

The Lyceum pantomime was strong in its homely tradition even down to the Harlequinade which, when I first went there, was still under one of the last of the great clown traditionalists—Whimsical Walker.

For three weeks before Christmas the old theatre would throb with the hubbub of its own technique and traditions. The book was written by the Brothers Melville; the Nephew of Sir Arthur was responsible for assembling the music which the theatre supplied, and he also checked the orchestral scores and parts contributed by individual artists. Principals arrived with their material intact and in many cases with their own wardrobes. Little Willie Clarkson with his tiny pinched-in waist, his rouged cheeks, top hat and frock coat —resembling a French barber in a comic opera—would trip round gesticulating and offering everyone costumes from his vast theatrical stores, known to the theatre world as Clarkson's. 'Wigs by Clarkson' was a byword in those theatre days and his own immaculate hair and trim beard were an excellent advertisement for his most famous contribution. He lived and breathed wigs, and complimented me on mine and asked me where I had got it; I had to explain, to his disappointment, that it had grown on my head. The Lyceum hardly rehearsed; it was a question of assimilation, and this went forward with speed and dexterity in every corner of the theatre.

I fell into the clutches of Madame Rosa, the ballet mistress. She was a minute little Jewess who had been quite a prominent dancer in the Alhambra ballets of the 'eighties. For me her fascination lay in the fact that she had been partly trained by the great Italian ballerina of those Alhambra days—Palladina. I never tired of asking her about her lessons with the Italian, but Madame Rosa mainly dwelt on the memory that the lessons had been very expensive; she said, however, that Palladina had a wonderful technique and was very popular in London. The Rosa had an elegant little black ebony ballet stick with a silver mount, no larger than a conductor's baton, her feet were tiny and beautifully formed; they were encased in very pointed, delicate shoes. She always wore a hat, a sort of cabbage toque which made the largest nose that I had ever seen seem even larger than it really was. She never took this hat off in the theatre, for someone had told her that with it on she resembled Queen Alexandra. She was very poor and lived all alone in a tiny flat in Long Acre; this was as near as she could get to the theatre world, and that world she had served from the age of five. In her room was a delicate painting of herself when young; it showed a *petite*, frail little person dominated by the nose and a pair of large piercing black eyes. On the last night of the pantomime she would grace the stage in an astounding Edwardian creation, an extremely low cut satin evening dress adorned with clumsy jewels. These jewels, she assured me, were gifts from the young bloods that frequented the Alhambra in her youth. It was known that every bracelet, necklace and brooch spent most of the year in pawn, but all were retrieved for this one spectacular appearance with their owner. She treated her 'ladies' as she called the *corps de ballet*—milling around in monotonous choreographic patterns— with great dignity, discipline, and frigid politeness. These ladies wore high heels, flowing Clarkson wigs and Clarkson dresses straight from the stores; they were buxom and heavily corseted, and they always carried some implement, for, as the Rosa would imply, they had no *port de bras*. Thus heavily camouflaged the ladies waltzed or pas-de-basqued their way through the fantastically pretty transformation scenes, parting suddenly to disclose the principal dancer.

The 'Grand Ballet' at the Lyceum was a spectacle that always ended the first half of the pantomime. It was as much a part of the tradition as the Harlequinade and was greeted with thunders of applause from an audience that would have known no bounds to its indignation if such a spectacle had been omitted. The end of the scene always found one standing in a golden chariot, or reposing on a cloud, or lying in a seashell, for the tableau was always a manifestation of the 'geographical' position of the pantomime; at that moment in time, it might be Dawn in a Garden of Flowers, Cloudland, or Under the Sea. The technique of the justly famed Transformation Scene never varied. A slow lifting of gauzes, a fading into scene after scene of fairylike splendour with miraculous lighting showing the splendours of the Lyceum's stage effects in that school of mechanical perfections belonging to the theatre of the Victorian era.

I can recall dashing Principal Boys, Fairy Godmothers with golden Clarkson tresses reaching to their knees, and endless streams of clowns and brilliant animal impersonators; pretty simpering

Principal girls, and hearty pantomime Dames with their red noses and topical jokes. I can hear the rafters echoing with the vibration of 'Keep the Home Fires Burning', the jokes about Zeppelins and Little Willie; there is also the memory of the nightly crossing of the Covent Garden Market in the First World War blackout.

The Lyceum was packed twice a day for about ten weeks; Drury Lane was the same. These two theatres held the London tradition of pantomime in their control, and their public could be counted on in the form of capacity houses throughout the run. I had a large fan mail that grew yearly; hundreds of the same people would be there every year in the same parties and sometimes on the same date. Anonymous gifts of jewellery, flowers and even crates of fruit would find their way to my dressing-room. The Lyceum was popular among the Canadian soldiers and the Anzacs from the Australian-New Zealand Army Corps. From such quarters came many of the most touching gifts that I received. Even today I receive a Christmas card from a faithful gallery fan of the Lyceum days; I have seen her, outside the stage door of Covent Garden, waiting for a glimpse of Dame Margot Fonteyn.

This yearly engagement for me was very fortunate; I was now studying very seriously with Espinosa who was ballet-master for a time at the Empire. I earned £5 a week at the Lyceum for my twelve performances, and I generally saved about £35 during the long run. The Brothers Melville were kindly, friendly creatures to meet, but they were notoriously close-fisted, and I had to supply costume, shoes and music. Salaries were paid in those days with a certain sense of the spectacular. I can still see Bill Hammond, the manager, in full evening tails and top hat, making the round of the theatre, with a tray hung from a strap round his neck. On this tray lay each artist's salary in a neat brown envelope; a rap on the dressing-room door, a slip of paper signed, a few friendly words exchanged, and you were left once more alone, but just that much richer than when you entered the theatre.

I managed, during those war years, to get an occasional concert engagement in the summer. To earn more money for my training,

I went to Eastbourne once every week to teach children for a well-known local instructor; I was well paid for the work, but it was strenuous. I gave half-hour private lessons from eleven o'clock in the morning until six-thirty in the evening. I then returned to London by a late train.

My training was quite expensive in comparison with the rate of living; two half-hour private lessons and one class every week cost me one guinea. I wrote all my lessons down, and executed them every day, sometimes for two hours at a stretch, for even at seventeen years of age I only had two to three hours' tuition per week. Week-ends were spent working in the kitchen of a military hospital in Park Lane. Later I was on the staff of the Victoria Station soldiers' canteen where I was eventually put in charge of a shift.

•   •   •

The war dragged on with its terrible toll of human life. My father was wounded in Gallipoli, and was later killed at Messines Ridge in the summer of 1917.

•   •   •

In the winter of '18 to '19 I fulfilled my last engagement at the Lyceum and was actually earning that year the princely salary of £10 a week. The war was over, the Russians were at the Coliseum, Cecchetti was teaching in London and had accepted me as a pupil.

My luck had changed; I had a good offer for a musical comedy that was to come to London in the spring and was to receive a salary of £16 a week.

Cecchetti taught in those days in a miserable place—the Chandos Hall. He was still with Diaghilev, both as artist and teacher, and so he did not have many pupils—about ten in all.

How fortunate were Cecchetti's first handful of pupils! I was one of them through the efforts of my last teacher—Hilda Bewicke. She had been a Russian-trained English member of the Diaghilev Com-

pany before the 1914 war, and was about to rejoin. I used to arrive
early for my class, so as to see the end of Lopokova's private lesson.
One morning she was executing a dance; her face was constrained
and anxious and the Maestro sent her back to the beginning again
and again. I discovered that I was actually seeing a pre-view of her
variation in *Boutique Fantasque*—the ballet that was shortly due to be
produced at the Alhambra Theatre. There was the day when Karsavina arrived among us, just after her escape from Russia: I can see
her breath-taking beauty as it struck me that morning on entering
the hall. She sat there with her small son and I thought of all the
most beautiful pictures of Madonnas that I had ever seen; I decided
that she was more beautiful than any of them.

This grim Chandos Hall could, at times, boast of rats in the
dressing-room: it was also the headquarters of the 'Bolshevik' Party
in London. Halls at that time were almost unprocurable, and the
moment arrived when the secretary of 'the Party' asked Cecchetti if
his pupils would dance for their fund-raising concert. The situation
was embarrassing—and the Maestro was frightened of losing the
hall. My childhood's deadly stubbornness returned, for I refused
point-blank to dance. I was shocked and angry and said that rather
than be blackmailed into doing this, we should be formed into groups
and go and look for another hall. An older student tried to reason
with me—using the argument that art might bring something into
these misguided people's minds . . . I'm afraid I retorted that our art
did not amount to enough to affect anyone's mind. I then had to
hear them tell the Maestro (when he asked about the programme)
that I 'would not dance for the Bolsheviks'. Awful pause; no comment; increased misery on my part coupled with a return of an
Irish sense of martyrdom. Most of my companions, mercifully, just
teased me; they took care to tell me, later, how everyone had sung
'The Red Flag': whereupon my political bias returned—fanned to
boiling point . . .

A vision of Madame Cecchetti: Tall, with a superb Edwardian carriage—she had a large head crowned with an astounding wig, which was worn well forward—resembling a furry toque; the colour was undoubtedly Madame's idea of the shade of her hair many, many years ago. She was the kindliest and sweetest of women. I always think of Madame sitting in a corner: she taught all the very young children (individually, all day long) in a corner of the studio. She never took up more than a few inches of the barre and a few feet of floor for her chair and the child; she would thus give a complete lesson from A to Z, changing her corner if necessary, yet remaining utterly oblivious of Maestro storming and whistling (we did quite a number of our exercises to lively extracts from *William Tell*).

As soon as any child was seen to be making any real progress (Madame was a wonderful teacher) Maestro would seize it and, in my opinion, set about ruining it; for this confiscation was embarked on far too early in the student's life.

If I ever had a reason to visit Maestro in his rooms in Soho's Wardour Street, I would find Madame in the sitting-room cooking his favourite Italian dishes—in a corner again, behind a tiny curtain. A large woman in a small space, she was always notably undisturbed by and detached from her surroundings; she appeared to be bent on the work on hand—a monument to capability, though never suffering from the faintest signs of inferiority. Time and again she would emerge from her various corners with the smooth progress of a Thames barge, chuckling and smiling; or she would sail forth resembling a slightly heavy fishing smack in tempestuous seas—to hold her own in an Italian domestic row (concerned possibly with too many changes of corner) of a not very silent order.

Lydia Lopokova, in spite of her two performances at the Coliseum and her heavy rehearsals for the coming Alhambra season, never missed her private lesson taken every morning at nine o'clock, before our class. She looked like an earnest tired child; her face had a grave sincerity, but when she laughed it was transformed; she suddenly resembled a hilarious cherub, or the God of Love himself in a mood that brooked no chain of restraint, for when Lopokova laughed she willed that the world laughed with her.

She had wonderful feet and the most beautiful hands, small and perfectly formed. But she would continuously draw attention to the individuality of her nose, and tell you with pride how an authoress, on account of this particular nose, had put her whole profile into a book. She jumped like a gazelle, giggled like a schoolgirl, and dramatized and projected every movement in class as she would in the theatre. No wonder she was tired; Lopokova, with all her lively wit, was as uninhibited as a fearless child, filled to the brim with the passing moment, and completely unconcerned about the future. Like a thunderclap she made one feel her capacity for direct thought. One was intensely aware of, and sometimes undermined by, her strong individuality; but it was an individuality divorced from any egotistical thought or action, for she had no vanity, no false pride— only a largesse of utter frankness and widespread generosity.

We students adored her, and she was particularly kind and helpful to me. Cecchetti would shout and scold at this diminutive dynamo and she would regard him, her small oval face fairly drooping with the gravity of the situation . . . then suddenly the air would be rent asunder by a peal of merriment that reduced the old Maestro to the growls of a distant ineffectual thunderstorm.

She showed oddity when it came to the buying of hats; I think that her preoccupation with her nose made her feel that a great frivolity in the millinery line was permissible. In the thirties she once told me how she arrived on the doorstep of 46 Gordon Square in a mad new creation from the Galeries Lafayette; the door opened and she was confronted by her husband. England's great economist stood rooted to the spot with horror at the sight of the millinery confection perched on the topmost point of his wife's small head. He gravely informed her that she must return with it at once to the shop—at once. She immediately obeyed and gave me later a philo-sophical enough explanation. She sensed that she had roused the fierce conventional spirit ever dormant in the soul of all Englishmen; on such occasions, she went on to reflect, her Imperial Ballet discipline would rear its head and she could but obey her husband's request, as she had once obeyed orders of like eccentricity on the part of the Director-Generals of the Imperial Court Theatres; obedience, she explained to me, at such baffling moments, became a conventional principle and must be recognized as the only possible solution; but, she added, she would always regret the loss of the beautiful chic little hat.

At Cecchetti's we met all the great dancers of the Diaghilev Ballet. I had suddenly travelled a very long way from the world of Mrs. Wordsworth, the theatre life of a children's touring company and the Lyceum pantomime.

.   .   .

Yet another break was in store for me. In this same summer of 1919, just one month before my twenty-first birthday, I crossed the Covent Garden market and exchanged the stage door of the Lyceum Theatre for the stage door of the Royal Opera House, Covent Garden.

After an audition, I found myself engaged at the Royal Opera House as *première danseuse* for the first post-war International Opera Season.

The Royal Opera House in 1919 was really the Royal Opera House of pre-war 1914, for the same customs and conventions held sway. The International Season of Grand Opera lasted from May to the end of July—a well planned festival covering a season of German, French and Italian Opera, with a galaxy of stars arriving from all parts of the globe. The Opera Ballet rehearsed in a room that is now the *corps de ballet's* dressing-room. We were under the direction of Monsieur Ambroisine, the ballet master from the Monnaie Theatre in Brussels. The Operas were produced by a Belgian named Ferdinand Almanz, who executed a form of Cook's tour of Opera Houses, stretching from Europe to South America. For every opera he had a highly efficient but limited series of gestures and static positions for individual singers and set groupings for choristers and supers; the speed of staging a work was quite fantastic, and dress rehearsals were practically unknown. I would be fitted for a costume, and wear it for the first time at the first performance. The prima donnas arrived with heavy trunk loads of complete wardrobes with them.

Two famous Italian costumiers were responsible for the actual Covent Garden Opera House wardrobes. They were called the brothers Comelli, and I never knew one from the other. Tall, fierce, autocratic and bad-tempered, they would stride about, permanently armed with minute designs of costumes in colour; complete down to the last detail, some of these designs and the realized costumes dated back thirty to fifty years. A design would be placed on your dressing-table on the night of the performance; the costume, itself removed from an outsize cardboard coffin, would hang in another part of the room, smelling strongly of moth balls. You then endeavoured, with the aid of design and dresser, to find space on your twentieth-century post-war five feet three inches of anatomy for a costume that resembled, in parts, a steelboned encasement, befitting the generous curves of the more statuesque nineteenth-century dancer. The Comellis could be adamant; at the original fitting, they would stand by and load you up; there was no escape—I would have to wait until the night of the performance when I would steal an opportunity to leave half my costume in the dressing-room.

The word of the brothers Comelli with the rank and file was law; they struck terror into the hearts of the wardrobe staff, likewise the chorus room and ballet room. They would be seen to creep round the wings hissing disapproval at some dancer or chorister and then rush off in search of stage directors and stir up an unhappy and tempestuous scene. They were always the Brothers Comelli; and you would say 'Here they come' even if it happened to be only one of them on the prowl.

A rehearsal on the stage of the Royal Opera House forty years ago was treated as an occasion. Convention decreed that ballet master or opera producer donned his hat and gloves and carried his walking stick when summoned with his flock on to the stage. The heads of the various stage departments wore long white coats as a mark of distinction; passing a room where several of these dignitaries might be in consultation always made me feel that an emergency surgical operation was about to begin.

The principal dressing-rooms were reached by means of a gangway in the wings of the prompt side. They resembled small Victorian bedrooms with heavy mahogany furniture and large swing mirrors.

I think that year was the only time that I saw the Opera House with all tiers filled by boxes. There was a great gala and in the Royal Box were King George V and Queen Mary, Queen Alexandra, the Prince of Wales, Princess Mary, and the young Dukes of York, Kent and Gloucester. In the light of subsequent history the Royal Box on that June night in 1919 held three kings who were to reign over England within the next eighteen years. I can see the boxes of the Diplomatic Corps round the same tier, each with some mark of distinction that I cannot now recall. . . . After my brief appearance in the Montmartre scene from *Louise* I went up into the flies with two young singers; one of them was Kathleen Destournel, who had just sung Musetta opposite Melba in a scene from *Bohème*, the other was a young singer full of her coming departure for Italy, where she hoped first to study and then to sing. Her name? Eva Turner. There stood the three of us, high up in the flies, peeping between the ropes at a scene of great brilliance and chattering about our futures.

Melba, Emma Destinn, Kirby Lunn, Elvira, Dinh Gilli, Tom Burke, they all flit across my memory . . . Melba on the gala night standing half-way up the dressing-room gangway complaining of feeling so tired and refusing any more autograph books. Sir Thomas Beecham, in defiance of bowlers, gloves and walking-sticks, conducting a rehearsal one morning with his coat off because of the heat. Herr Almanz sticking my head firmly on the chest of the tenor playing the 'Pape des Fous' in *Louise* and forgetting to remove it. I was too terrified to do anything about it, and the young French tenor quite obviously did not want our position subjected to any modification.

My dresser was a Mrs. Harris, who, with her sister, the head wardrobe mistress, had been at Covent Garden for nearly fifty years.

When the curtain descended on the last night of the International season these two, with one assistant, would start to go through the great opera wardrobe cupboards, one by one, in preparation for what might be required out of that vast store the following year.

I once asked Mrs. Harris how they knew that they were keeping up to schedule; Mrs. Harris informed me that if they had reached the Faust angel wings in her moth hunt round about Easter, all was well . . . Mrs. Harris was known, with great respect, as Tetrazzini's Favourite Dresser, and this became indeed a form of address more usual than Mrs. Harris.

I was still dancing in a musical comedy at the Strand, and was released for the nights that I was required at the Opera. By August the Opera was finished but not my other engagement. I was very much alone in London and Cecchetti was faced with only one pupil to teach. It was then that the Maestro gave me a series of gruelling but wonderful private lessons. He was a great teacher; he had a special system, which, in my opinion, possibly cramped his full powers. He had many sound theories that will live for ever as a part of all ballet teaching, and he had other theories that are already discarded. He was a great mime of the old school; but although he had been a famous virtuoso dancer he demanded grace from women before anything else. Unity of movement was a fetish with him; I have seen him hurl both abuse and his stick at a dancer who attempted to learn a step by executing it only from the waist down. He would always prefer first to be given the proof by his pupil of some knowledge pertaining to the head and body movements . . . thus we were expected to master the épaulement first, even to the point of sometimes marking the step with our hands.

As a character he was, to say the least, all Italian; that terrible book he kept with our names written in one long neat row! On occasions this record was opened out in front of the whole class and everyone was gently made aware of who had not paid, and gravely a mark was put against the name—and the book would then be closed with a telling sigh.

With the help of Madame Cecchetti he would teach all day; between them they ran an ever increasing and lucrative school.

Towards the end of their sojourn here the old gentleman had much trouble with the Income Tax authorities. Although he was able to send large sums of money back to Italy, it was quite beyond his understanding that something was also owing to the English Inland Revenue.

The kindly father of an English pupil who offered to help, rued that day to the bitter end; the Maestro would inform him gravely and grandly that he had a great respect for the English law and was quite prepared to give the Commissioner of Taxes—£5. It was common knowledge that he was making about £100 per week. But no proper books were kept and the Maestro's French disappeared; with great heat and speed he would argue exclusively in his native Italian . . .

Maestro Cecchetti left a great imprint on the English School, and was my exclusive teacher for four years. The important aspects of his teaching will remain a part of the academic tradition of our English ballet. In his own right he had been a great artist, both as a mime and a virtuosity dancer. Few realize that he was the first to dance the 'Blue Bird' in Russia. In directions that were unexpected he showed a shrewd appreciation of talent. He worshipped Pavlova, but he had no respect for a technician with little else to offer outside his technical feats; as a great exponent of the Italian School of precision and virtuosity this attitude made him unique. I imagine that it was partly the result of his long stay in Russia; later again there was the influence of the years spent with the Diaghilev Company. Up to the end of Cecchetti's life Diaghilev would continually persuade him to take over the perfecting of young dancers in the company who he considered needed the Maestro's special system.

Cecchetti never produced a ballerina solely trained under his method. This was a criticism levelled at his teachings by many great dancers, and I would say that the comment is not an unfair one. He undoubtedly had a genius for giving a dancer a certain stamp and finish; he also had (through certain aspects of his special system) a great capacity for correcting a serious fault. It is recorded that he taught Pavlova exclusively for two years in Russia; Pavlova's intention was that he should eradicate a certain fault in her work that he had mentioned to her at their first meeting.

He would make many wise observations—professional conclusions arrived at through a lifetime wholly lived in the theatre. He said that there was no such thing as a *prima ballerina* under the age of twenty-six years, but that there was nothing more beautiful to see in life than the same in embryo in her late teens or very early twenties. He declared that every great dancer needed a special highlight in her work to give her individual distinction; he hinted that the possible emphasis should fall on one of the following: elevation, pirouettes, or line.

Maestro Cecchetti finished his long life in a great theatre that he had so much desired to serve; during the last few years of his life he was appointed *maitre de ballet* to La Scala, Milan . . . he died of a heart attack in that Opera House one morning where he had gone, as usual, to take his daily class.

His was an end that any artist might well choose.

Within the London studio of the Maestro, where the great and small studied, I continued to work for the next few years.

It was in the autumn of 1921 that Diaghilev presented his famous revival of *The Sleeping Beauty*; night after night it was possible to watch the performances of a group of distinguished ballerinas. Spessitziva, Trefilova, Egorova were the original three Princesses and later Lopokova and Nemchinova both appeared in the role. The London public in general was apathetic; the comparatively small coterie of followers that Diaghilev had for his modern works would support him handsomely for a six weeks' season, but without wider public support, a three months' season of one full length ballet was doomed to meet with disaster. England did not have the great ballet public of today and classical ballet of such dimensions was unknown.

The failure of this sumptuous spectacle resulted in Diaghilev's departing penniless for Paris. The Company was stranded in London. On the last sad night, to a house full of faithful followers, Lopokova in a brave little curtain speech announced that they would soon return, 'very good-humoured ladies'. But everyone knew that the situation was serious; in fact, England did not see the Russian Ballet again until the winter of 1924, by which time I was a member of the Company.

In retrospect, I regard the failure of the Diaghilev *Sleeping Beauty* as of secondary importance when compared with the interest that it aroused in traditional classical ballet: it could be said that the seed of true appreciation had been sown in a minority of the slow-but-sure British public, but it was a minority that remained steadfast and faithful to this new aspect of the ballet.

•   •   •

For me the weaving of a pattern continued; over a span of nearly twenty years *The Sleeping Beauty* had yet again aroused me to an awareness of the Princess Aurora's wondrous beauty . . .

Covent Garden Opera House enters my life for the second time. Leonide Massine arrived in England in the late autumn of 1921 and started a small company consisting of the then out-of-work Diaghilev stars. The group consisted of Lopokova, Sokolova, Woizikowski, Slavinsky, Savina, and a few extra dancers—of whom I was one.

It was my first contact with Russian Ballet; the choreography was of an order undreamt of in any of my previous experiences, and the disciplined routine of class and lengthy rehearsals in preparation for the opening filled me with a sudden feeling of dedication that was an entirely new sensation.

This atmosphere was enhanced by the fact that I had just finished an engagement on a music-hall circuit in which I had attempted to present some ten English dancers in a twenty minutes' *divertissement,*

MME ADELINE GENEE, D.B.E.
(1902)

PHYLLIS BEDELLS IN
'THE BELLE OF THE BALL',
EMPIRE THEATRE

MRS. WORDSWORTH

'THE DYING SWAN' (1912)

THE LILA FIELD ACADEMY, 1912 (The Author fourth from left)

with all the choreography arranged by myself. It had been mildly successful, and the end of the venture after six weeks was mainly due to a very serious slump in the variety theatres.

The Massine-Lopokova Company had to present a new set of *divertissements* every week in support of a film; a film to be shown at the Opera House. This new venture meant that the Covent Garden syndicate was exploring another means of reducing the expense of a closed Opera House for nine months out of the year.

But the experiment failed; within one month Covent Garden resolutely closed its doors to films.

Sir Oswald Stoll moved the Russian dancers to the Coliseum. I was fortunate enough (through the request of Lopokova—the best friend of my life in the theatre) to be given the opportunity of continuing with them.

It was Sir Oswald who was responsible for an almost immediate return to the Opera House.

Within a few weeks an American producer, in association with Sir Oswald, took the Opera House to stage a spectacle that bore the challenging title of *You'd Be Surprised*, further clarified under the hideous description of 'Jazzaganza'. What it amounted to was a very indifferent revue led by George Robey. It did, though, attempt to live up to its crazy title, for it harboured, amid comedians and chorus girls, a ballet choreographed by Massine, with music by Darius Milhaud, and scenery and costumes by Duncan Grant. It was danced by Massine and Lopokova, Woizikowski and Sokolova, Slavinsky and myself. I can remember little about it except that I was dressed as a piccaninny, my face blackened, and with Slavinsky, executed an intensely difficult duet dance.

The Jazzaganza was a loosely constructed entertainment presenting a collection of English and American revue stars. Much indignation was expressed as to the propriety of such an activity entering the portals of the Royal Opera House. Rumours of a demonstration on the part of the gallery made the prospect of first night nerves even more of a certainty than the poorness of the book had already inspired.

5

George Robey, however, made an impromptu entrance on that
nerve-racking first occasion: it was an entrance that routed the
trouble-mongers on the immediate rise of the curtain.

With his finger on his lips he tiptoed straight down to the footlights; the eyebrows were raised higher than ever, but quizzically
asymmetrical in their mock-agitation—'Hush, hush,' he announced,
'you mustn't laugh here . . .'

Covent Garden Opera House was again to stand for no nonsense;
for one month the walls disdainfully supported her vast internal plush
and gilded disapproval; at the end of that time, the ballet scene was
cancelled and the whole revue, with its tail not only lowered but
considerably curtailed, removed itself to the Alhambra Theatre,
where it was to play three times a day: the arrangement definitely
smacked of penance.

I was offered a fresh contract by the Stoll management to stay on
and dance in two of the revue scenes; and so I continued at the
Leicester Square Theatre throughout the late spring and summer of
'22.

•   •   •

Sandwiched in those years between 1917 and 1923 I had many an
experience of the old-fashioned type of English music-hall, as well
as the more opulent modern examples. I appeared at most of the
Gulliver Circuit Halls, in and around the suburbs of London, where
there were always twice-nightly performances. I have also danced at
the Old Oxford, the Holborn Empire, the Palladium, and often (in
varied company) at the London Coliseum. The Palladium was the
most exacting—with its three performances a day; I remember
dancing there during the First World War (I forget the year) when
I appeared for two weeks with a Belgian dancer, Robert Roberty—
famed for his brilliant pirouettes; he could average twelve to four-
teen turns. I can recall many of my fellow artists: Ella Shields, whose
incredible rendering of 'Burlington Bertie' is with me to this day—
Little Tich, Grock, Wee Georgie Wood—they pass in a procession
before my eyes with their kindly comradeship, their easy professional

handling of the noisy, adoring audience which was theirs—whether at the Palladium, Coliseum, or one of the more rough and ready outer halls. Monday morning rehearsals for these established favourites did not exist, for the staffs of the music-halls were familiar with the presentation of the respective acts of these artists: time and again they would play two and three 'halls' the same week—travelling to and fro in full stage costume and make up every evening: thus they would give four to six performances between 6 p.m. and midnight.

The music-hall scene on Monday mornings I conjure up as the origin of all Crazy Gangs. Orchestra, sets, lighting, tumblers, vocalists, dancers, trick cyclists, acrobats, wire walkers—all that went to make up the hurly-burly of 'the Bill' became like a congested circus ring. The orchestral players were always rather bad, but, nevertheless, obliging; it appeared to me that the players were in the habit of taking charge of the conductor. An orchestral introduction to a comedian's 'business' was known as 'till-readies' . . . it went on, a tiny, monotonous little rhythm, until its abrupt termination burst on everyone by means of an arranged signal from the red-nosed, baggy-trousered little funny man. Control of such technicalities was the main function of the conductor, who otherwise—once he had started the orchestra playing—did very little more until he had to stop them: there is the true story of an aggrieved old orchestral player who reprimanded a zealous new conductor at a London music-hall with the following: 'Hi, guv'nor, with us—if you please.'

I knew the dread, in my music-hall days, of the provincial Monday night second-house audience: in those days it was an old music-hall tradition to give all turns a rough reception at that particular performance—it was never vindictive, but disturbing indeed would be the laughs, whistles and cat-calls that greeted every turn all over the country throughout the entertainment world on a Monday night second house.

In the autumn of 1918 I found myself at the Palladium in the more secluded and protected society of the Beecham Opera Company.

Sir Thomas Beecham's effort for English Opera came at an unfortunate moment in history, but to add to the irony of the situation, it was a rich period in the history of English operatic talent. The Palladium season was an attempt to provide a half-hour entertainment of opera and ballet, as a means of giving employment (between tours) to the chorus and the ballet; I had joined the latter as a guest artist just for four weeks. I can remember a ballet to a suite of Bach arranged by Goossens, with scenery and costumes by Edmond Dulac; the choreography, alas, was by anyone—I had to arrange my own dances. The second act of *Carmen* was given with the ballet and we also presented the full *Faust* ballet. The Brothers Comelli, of course, held sway over the costumes.

An interesting example of the strength of the Beecham Opera Company lay in the four conductors who took it in turn to conduct these opera ballets; the performances were divided among Percy Pitt, Eugene Goossens, Julius Harrison and Leslie Heward. With the exception of the mature Percy Pitt, here indeed was an avalanche of young conductors of note. I appeared with the Company once again, in de Lara's *Naïel*, which was given three performances by the Beecham Company during the International Season at Covent Garden the following year.

•   •   •

For nearly three years my life had been spent in West End revues and music-halls; I had reached saturation point and a dangerous state of boredom. I was hopelessly dissatisfied with my new rôle in the Alhambra revue, an engagement that demanded my presence in the theatre from noon to midnight.

My only interest, while at the Alhambra, was that every morning I went to Hampstead to study with Legat—for Cecchetti had returned to Italy. But even the full benefit of my lessons with Legat (for me an intensely stimulating teacher, whose style was exactly what I, schooled in Italian precision, needed to round off my studentship) was hampered by my three performances every day.

I was getting physically exhausted and in a very unprofitable way.

How fortunate it was that my brief period in the company of those Russian dancers, in their miniature ballet productions, had ruined me for my present surroundings. I had known for some time that Diaghilev had started up again in France, for most of my Russian friends of the past year had rejoined him. The Russian Company, as it happened, required another young classical dancer; those members of the Company whom I had worked with and others who remembered seeing me at Cecchetti's classes, spoke to Diaghilev about me. Cecchetti's opinion was sought in Italy—and Grigorieff was instructed to have a conversation with me in London.

Their united recommendations were enough: without having to face one of those dreaded auditions I actually received an offer to join the Russian Ballet.

September 1923 found me rehearsing in Paris with my new companions.

III

THE EXTENDED CIRCLE

... 'Have you noticed,' he said, 'that up to now you have always been in the *centre* of the circle? Yet you may sometimes find yourself outside. For example—

'Everything became dark; then a ceiling light, in the next room, was lighted, throwing a spot on the white tablecloth and the dishes.

'Now you are beyond the limits of the small circle of your attention. Your rôle is a passive one; one of observation. As the circle of light is extended and the illuminated area in the dining-room grows, your circle also becomes larger and larger, and the area of your observation increases in the same ratio. Also you can use the same method of choosing points of attention in these circles that lie behind you.'

CONSTANTIN STANISLAVSKY, *An Actor Prepares*

M Y YEARS with the Diaghilev Russian Ballet have been briefly recorded in another book. The day by day life in that Company has no place in this autobiography: like other scenes those years will be compressed into a general impression of a certain period of time.

If one is fortunate—and many of us have more good fortune than we recognize—there are certain stretches of time in life which are sharply isolated; forever such moments stand apart from the general landscape, for in retrospect we see that they awoke new perceptions within us, resulting in an up-grading of our sensibility and a fundamental change in our outlook. We experience our own glimpse of 'a world in a grain of sand' and a passage of time may be needed before we are able to express this awareness. Our intelligence guards this thing patiently, surrounding it with an invisible mesh that preserves it for future use.

We all appear to have an inner life that is expressed, to some extent, by its diverse interests. In the case of many people, it is difficult to associate these interests with the normal tenor of their lives. The mass mind has invented for these cases the explanatory title of escapism, disregarding the fact that acquisition of a special knowledge can lead to a life entirely dedicated to a certain interest.

There follow the recognizable forms of specialization: There is the man who learns solely for the development of his own aesthetic sense, and he, on a higher plane, becomes a connoisseur; there is the man who is inspired to express learning in a creative form—the artist;

there is he who probes for a reasoned and eclectic understanding—. the scholar.

If we think upon distinguished upholders of learning, we note evidence of combinations of the above often present in the one person: the connoisseur who develops into a scholar; the creative artist whose discernment also points to a connoisseur; the scholar who possesses the creative impulse . . .

What happens when we find the connoisseur, the creator and the scholar in one person? I say that we have a wholly unusual mind at work in a certain creative form—and it is thus that I see Diaghilev in retrospect.

To feel one's values and standards undergo a complete change is an extraordinary sensation. It was through Diaghilev that I became aware of a new world, a world that held the secrets of that aesthetic knowledge that I sought, but which showed me that further discoveries would need a divergent approach if I were to attain any knowledge of these principles. In him I encountered a higher form of genius, a state of mind capable of concerning itself with the basic principle of perfect unity in a creative work. There must be moments of revelation to enable such people to perceive consistently the beauty and power of order. They see artists wrapt in their isolated interests— and with invisible strings they draw them together and co-ordinate the whole.

Theirs is not the emotion experienced by the individual aesthete, it is rather the emotion that guides the path of aestheticism in general.

•   •   •

The Russian Ballet in Western Europe was a facet of a great traditional theatre ballet that had been nourished within the frame of the Russian theatre in general. Through the remarkable vision of Diaghilev this facet was remoulded into a complete unit.

His group of artists, musicians and dancers succeeded in portraying a complete Russian picture; in style they had their classical tradition of the ballet as handed to them in the past by the great schools of Western Europe. In presentation they had their own Russian tradition of dance and folklore in its limitless richness of pattern and subject matter.

The personnel consisted of artists who could be likened to a younger generation of any community of people interpreting the traditions of an art form. In Russia there was little room for these artists; the great machine that had made them was overloaded, and, to their young and alert minds, it was in a rut. In a sense they were right, for such a machine must inevitably be concerned with the traditional whole, and the preservation of the pedagogy inherent in such backgrounds.

But for the advent of Diaghilev, these artists would have drifted abroad individually, merely to be swallowed up by institutions not unlike their own at home. What was done was of great significance to the traditional Russian Ballet: a fraction of its younger generation was preserved intact—dancers, composers, choreographers—with their disciplined background as their foundation stone. At the pinnacle of this new order was Diaghilev, welding, moulding, guiding and seeking.

It is hard to imagine what would have influenced the English and American Schools of Ballet had it not been for the 1914 war and the Russian Revolution. Before 1914 the Diaghilev Company paid only annual visits to Europe; the artists had to obtain leave of absence from both the St. Petersburg and the Moscow Imperial Theatres. Eventually the war and the revolution found many of the artists willing exiles, turning to Diaghilev to mould their future lives.

By 1919, the exotic, perennially flowering branch of a great tree trunk—a branch yearly carried to Europe—was in one sense gone. There could be no return for another spring's flowering. It became imperative for Diaghilev to transplant this cutting and see that it took root and grew afresh in foreign soils.

I was lucky inasmuch as I was with this Company when the impact of the present was meeting the past. I saw both worlds, and very much from a position of passive observation. What a revelation it was for one who had, first by the teachings of Cecchetti and Legat, and then by the Massine-Lopokova Company, at last reached a part of the core of Russian Ballet!

For the first time in my life I sensed a condition of world theatre. In addition, all Europe was before my eyes; its cities, museums, art galleries, its customs and its theatres. Everything merged into a whole—a city's architecture became inseparable from the ballet, and the ballet itself was moulding me as part of a future that was a development of the past. A spirit of tradition was at work, with a heritage so rich that one knew its transplantation to new soil would be possible time and again.

The fire, however, was not lit with the speed of the recorded history; at first there had to be an acceptance in part; for deep concentration on immediate tasks was asked of me; much pre-occupation also with the assimilation of style; a gradual approach was essential, so as to understand eventually the intricate material that formed the background to everything.

Like all great minds, Diaghilev respected all people and things functioning in their proper sphere: and as his sense of proportion was as impeccable as his taste, Diaghilev lived beyond the world of his artists. He was concerned with the development of Russian traditions. His strength lay in the fact that his familiarity with the value of the known and the tried was so great that he could advise with conviction and discard with impunity; he could light the path of the unknown and untried with the torch of experience.

As a result of his upbringing and his country's theatrical history, he had a deep-rooted veneration for the orthodox. I can recall his excitement when he received an engagement for the Company to appear at La Scala, Milan. It was the summer of 1926 and although by then I had left the Russian Ballet, he asked me to promise him that I would travel to Milan in the following January to dance two variations in *Aurora's Wedding*. When I hesitated, he became both agitated and persuasive, emphasising that I would be able to say I had danced at La Scala.

The above reflection compels me to make a short digression at this point on the subject of the Diaghilev Exhibition of 1954, in London and Edinburgh.

In spite of the superb examples of his life's work, I feel that the presentation would have irritated Diaghilev; the Exhibition, in its visual decorations, did not present the man as the autocrat of taste that he was to those who knew him. One never failed to sense his habitual love of ritual and tradition, however preoccupied he was with the *avant garde* of Paris. I feel that he would have preferred his exhibition to have been held in one of our National Galleries, without the Madame Tussaud effects to which it was subjected. It was thought to be something that he would have liked, something, I heard said, that would have appealed to his humour . . . but I know something of Russian humour, which has a little in common with the Irish brand: it is singularly capable of not being amused, with the frozen countenance of a Queen Victoria.

A dual personality was, of course, often at work in Diaghilev, and all the examples of his worst side were concerned with the futile. Such futility, even if only hinted at, inclines to misrepresentation. He was by nature autocratic, proud and conservative; and the values that he left to the world of art show only a mind of great culture, with its disciplined background of the orthodox.

•   •   •

Slowly the essence of the Russian Ballet worked on me as I learnt to adapt myself to my new surroundings. All facets were visible to me, but for a time they stood out with a sharp singularity of purpose; their relation to each other was hidden from me, the final pattern obscured, yet I sensed the magnitude of the reward that was to be found eventually in the completed picture. I soon sensed the feel of the sharp line of division between examples of pedagogy in academic study and choreography on the stage; it could be likened to an understanding of the difference between prose and poetry.

I was first to contend with the discovery of certain trends in relation to my own work. It was brought home to me that I was a 'quick study' with a facility for absorbing the required style and characterization of a rôle; I was musical by Russian standards, and had, in the opinion of my fellow artists, a considerable and very accurate technique. But my projection and general attack were faint in comparison with the Russians, my personality reserved, and stamina (outside technical feats) for the hardship of the life—low.

I feel that some of the above remarks represent a possible comparison between any English and Russian artist. Russians can be physically indefatigable; they can also be astonishingly inaccurate in their repetition of any set movement, and thus, the sustaining of Russian vitality is free from the tiring restraint of discipline and accuracy: they are consistently concerned with the uninhibited projection of themselves. It must be admitted that sometimes projection of energy is not, with Russian dancers, always distributed equally between the physical and the mental; there is, more than often, a magnificent dynamic offering in one or the other direction: the banks may be flooded over, adding dramatic effect to the landscape. This gives much exhilaration and pleasure to witness, provided that you do not happen to be something on the bank . . .

I once danced the rôle of one of the two nymphs in *Narcisse and Echo*; my partner was a dancer whose performance in any of the Russian national dances was the essence of a dynamic inherent musicality. In this particular ballet, Fokine's conception of the relationship between music and step was not complicated. I had found it easy to learn and just as easy to remember. My companion, however, gave her own interpretation (always a good one) at every performance; it varied in accent and beat and ignored the basic reading; for the choreographer's fundamental fusion of music and step did not appear to have made any impression on her. Quickly I realized that the situation was quite beyond my control; I threw my hand in and became her unacknowledged accompanist.

• • •

What a deep-rooted theatre sense there was in the work of those four distinguished choreographers, Fokine, Massine, Nyjinska and Balanchine. These artists were the architects of the lines of development that Diaghilev presented throughout the twenty-five years of the ballet's life.

In all four cases more was involved than the hand of Diaghilev: the roots from which they had had to cut themselves off still had their deep significance . . . for the artists, as for Diaghilev, it was the march of progress evolving from all that had gone before.

Fokine, the great romantic traditionalist of the Russian Ballet theatre, with *Les Sylphides* to the music of Chopin, showed a faultless conception of romanticism, founded in every respect on a great tradition. Today this work stands supreme as an example of its style in contemporary ballet; it was Diaghilev's favourite.

Through the creations of Massine, I witnessed Diaghilev's first preoccupation with the Western European theatre. The choreographic development of the character dance in ballet was here fused with the theatre to some real effect; it was no longer an isolated form of dance. Character work, including the basic elements of national dances, underwent at this period of the Diaghilev Russian Ballet a great reformation. It could be likened to the fate of 'mime', which had already subjected itself to development far removed from the conventional gestures that had been, in the past, its sole form of expression.

The intricate and often asymmetrical fusion of body movement with steps is to be noted in the choreography of Massine; this led in the end to an increased understanding of the control of movement. I think that the study of Massine movement, through the medium of his ballets choreographed in the 1920's, is of immense importance to young artists today, dealing as they do mainly with the neo-classical contemporary works. It was Nyjinska and Balanchine who first concerned themselves with neo-classicism; here again we witness the work of two artists who had been steeped in the learnings of a great tradition. The neo-classicism of the later Diaghilev period has been absorbed and digested in the last twenty years: it has even presented its points of value to the main stream of the classical ballet of today, showing signs of having served its time and purpose as an isolated 'ism'.

Slowly this kaleidoscope settled itself before my bewildered eyes: the world that I had lived in fell away . . . and with the impatience of youth, I found myself drawn towards an extreme point of view in relation to my sense of aesthetic appreciation at the time.

I will give two examples of this aesthetic upheaval, for both of them stand out with singular clarity in my mind.

I was alone in my dressing-room early one morning at the Champs-Elysées Theatre. Through the loudspeaker on the wall came the strains of a full orchestral and choral rehearsal of *Les Noces* under the baton of Stravinsky. Up to that moment I had not seen or rehearsed this work, neither had the Company spoken of it with any particular awe—except in relation to its difficulties. Rooted to the spot, I was emptied of every thought: the music and the voices held me in a vice. I felt that I was present at a mystical revelation of the soul of a country, a pagan ritual concerned with primeval joy and sorrow.

The rehearsals that followed, with a nervous company refreshing their memories and endeavouring to teach me the difficult rhythms, increased my feeling of exaltation, and I took away copious notes to memorize. From this detailed study was to emerge a clear picture of the geometrical beauty of the inner structure and relationship between the music and the choreography.

THE AUTHOR AGED 16

AGED 17

MME ROSA, 1914.   THE LYCEUM
THEATRE'S BALLET MISTRESS

LYDIA LOPOKOVA IN 'THE GOOD HUMOURED LADIES' (1919)

I heard later that when Diaghilev first witnessed one of the early rehearsals of this ballet, he left without making any criticism: it was said that he had never been known to be so completely satisfied with any ballet in its embryo state.

My other sharply outlined recollection is the revival of *Le Lac des Cygnes* at Monte Carlo, with Madame Vera Trefilova as guest artist. The work of the *corps de ballet* was painstakingly revived by those members of the Company who had been in the Imperial Ballet. I found myself uninterested; the ballet and the music struck me as old-fashioned and boring. It took Trefilova to save me from complete disillusionment: here I certainly sensed the greatness of the execution and the perfection of the central structure of the ballet.

In a way I was not altogether to blame; in my raw state it was difficult to develop a sense of proportion at a time when the relationship between the modern and the classical ballet was less close than it is today. In the staging of a modern production, I was used to the highest contemporary standards in dancing, décor, costumes and music; alongside this state of perfection, I was confronted with a very indifferent and abbreviated classical revival; by our standards of today the *corps de ballet* had not the high classical efficiency of dancing that is found in modern companies. The Diaghilev Ballet of my time was mainly a group of first dancers and soloists; the actual *corps* was very uneven, and not well balanced as a whole.

It took time for me to understand the influence of the classical tradition on the Company's work; enlightenment did not come until after I had left, and I had found time to reflect on the whole experience.

• • •

Life with my fellow artists was colourful. To a native of Ireland the pattern did not strain, nor did my state of exile tug at my heart strings and produce a nostalgia for the theatre friends that I had left in England.

We hear much of artists' love of freedom; yet artists in daily contact with each other (as in the case of a ballet company) present an example of a rigid code of discipline and community life carried to fantastic lengths. It can be compared with the circumscribed world of a university, and is just as much isolated from everyday reality.

I had lived a much freer existence in the theatre world of England: yet that freedom, in comparison with the strict discipline imposed on me now, was empty and unproductive; it had been lonely and without purpose, and had failed to illuminate either the present or the future.

To understand fully the Russian Ballet theatre life one has to remember that the artists had lived cloistered lives in the Russian State Schools; now they were further bound together by the *émigré* spirit, cut off as they were from the land of their birth, and served with passports issued from Geneva. Their predicament made them either expansive or reticent. They seemed to carry their lives on their backs, a mental and emotional knapsack, stuffed with memories of the past, anxiety about the present, and hopes for the future. I noticed that the entire ballet company would drift back to the South of France for the holidays, to places associated with months of hard work; these places, for them, held neither roots nor interests, their attraction, I imagine, lay in a certain air of familiarity.

England they all seemed to love and they appeared to regard our land as a country possessing a superior form of happiness. I sensed, however, that their affection for my country had no connection with pleasure: they felt that England offered security. Later, most of them were to find this security in the United States.

I, on my side, puzzled them. They insisted that I was so much more like them than the other English members of the Company. Of course their experience of English artists was very limited; I doubt if more than ten English dancers became permanent members of the Russian Ballet in the twenty years of its existence. Yet there was some foundation for their remark, for my Celtic blood had far more in common with theirs than that of any other artist of a purer English strain. They were very frank in their wish to thrash this matter out one day: the discussion took place on a long train journey. I became heavily involved in stating the case of the Irish and succeeded in clarifying the situation only when I said that to call an Irishman an Englishman was as incorrect as to call a Russian a Pole!

In Berlin, an English correspondent of the *Daily Mail* brought a friend to a dress parade of *Cimarosiana*, held in the foyer of the Opera House. He told me later that he had asked his friend to observe the girl in front of the mirror—she was such a perfect example of the Slav type—and at that moment my attention was withdrawn from the mirror, and I called out to someone at a distance—in English. . . .

The Company held many true Dostoievsky or Tchekov-like characters. Patient, aristocratic *émigrés* such as Prince A. Shervashidze who painted scenery for Diaghilev; conservative and enchanting Alexander Benois, who designed for some of the Operas in Monte Carlo; the Polunins, who later settled in England, where Vladimir Polunin became teacher of the Continental style of scenic painting at the Slade School. Those two great artists Larianov and Goncharova were also, from time to time, a part of the Russian ballet scene. Diaghilev found all these artists work, but life for them must have been hard and uncertain; their distinctive Russian style of painting was not suited to the ballets of that period, concerned as Diaghilev was by then with works of artists from Western Europe.

Occasionally a young dancer from some part of Russia would join us: we had one girl who came straight from the Leningrad School and another from Moscow, but neither of them showed any unusual talent. Four boys arrived from Kiev—young, raw and very inexperienced. Their lives and consequently their health had suffered much hardship; they seemed particularly young for their age and rather undersized: Serge Lifar was one of this quartet.

The most exciting little group of *émigrés* to join us, however, was the Balanchine-Gevergeeva-Danilova-Efimov quartet. We were in London at the time, dancing at the Coliseum during the Christmas period of 1924. One Sunday morning I was summoned to Astafieva's studio with about six other artists. Balanchine was there, young and anxious-looking. He had an engaging charm and a great sense of humour which had made him popular with us, although he had only been with the company for about ten days. His dancing had proved to be rather less than indifferent, but we suspected in him some other form of distinctive talent. For two solid hours we learnt a choreographic conception of his, set to a Funeral March . . . (I never hear this music without calling to mind that Sunday morning). I worked with a will, for I was as acutely aware as others of his gifts. Just about midday Diaghilev, Kochno and Grigorieff arrived, and we went through our choreographic patterns. On such occasions Diaghilev was an enigma. Face impassive, manner aloof; we were all robots, from Balanchine downwards, and there was no means of fathoming the impression made on our director. I knew that a rumour was circulating in the company that Nyjinska was leaving us quite soon, and that the young Balanchine might become our new choreographer.

The winter season that followed in Monte Carlo, found him in charge of the Opera ballets that we had to dance every year. How refreshing was his originality! I can remember taking part in many small duets and ensembles arranged by him in the various operas: he charged these dreary experiences with a new life and interest, and no demands on him could curb his imaginative facility. His great musical sense never failed to make the most of the material offered to him, even when confronted with that outlet so universally dreaded by all choreographers—the opera-ballet.

I do not think that the life we led would be very popular among repertory ballet artists of today. By comparison it was certainly very much harder, and I doubt whether, if ballet had been in the strong position that it is today, Diaghilev could have kept his company together, except with a greatly changed order of things on the domestic front.

In retrospect, the work of Grigorieff, the general manager, was monumental. I was very fond of him and had an intense admiration for his integrity, intelligence and kindliness. It was, however, quite beyond his power to lessen the evils of overwork, or the lack of thought at the top for a company's minor comforts or even, on occasions, the lack of encouragement.

To give a small example of the domestic disorder that aroused my English spirit of justice: we might be summoned to dance after midnight at a big French reception during the height of the summer season; this was fair enough, as Diaghilev needed such lucrative engagements. The question of transport home at 3 a.m., however, meant that the artists were faced individually with taxi charges at about four times their day-rate. On our modest salaries this was out of the question. I can recall walking from the Champs-Elysées halfway back to the Boulevard St. Germain, because I could not afford a taxi the whole way; this walk came as the climax of a day's work that had started the previous morning at 9 a.m.; we were fined if we missed the early morning class.

In comparison with today, how different was the treatment of artists! I cannot recall, at any of those great functions, receiving any civility or hospitality from anyone . . . on the contrary I can still feel my worry and consternation when I missed the backstairs in some large house facing on to a moonlit garden and found myself caught on the front stairs—surrounded by Paris *en grand gala*. The matter greatly agitated me; there was the thought that Diaghilev would see me, and that he would be angry for two reasons—my presence on the wrong staircase and the fact that my well-worn *Sylphides* costume would be ill-met by anything but moonlight. At these galas we were never given anything to eat or drink; it is fair, though, to admit that I was the only one to express irritation. My companions, I imagine, were used to this treatment outside England; in time they listened to my indignant outbursts with a certain interest and slowly awakening curiosity.

I obtained a minor reaction on their part, however, at the opening of the new Galeries Lafayette. The whole of the centre of the main shop had been turned most ingeniously into a theatre. By means of a lift we were transported from the attics (where we dressed) to the first floor where a stage had been erected. The attics were prim, bare little rooms, used by the shop girls, with rows of little tin wash-basins. Beside each little basin was an elegant cake of soap and an attractive hand towel. We waited a long time: it was well into the early hours of the morning before we had finished—foodless and drinkless as usual. In my extreme state of tiredness I held forth as to my opinion of French shop-owners in general. I then suggested that, as a mild protest, we should go home with all that we could lay hands on—soap and the towels. We did. For two days I cherished the hope that there would be a public reprimand for petty larceny, but I was to be disappointed. There was no complaint and therefore no opportunity (as I imagined) to awaken Diaghilev to the unsatisfactory state of our social welfare!

Outstanding was our one true Dostoievsky character—the Company's wigmaker. Silent and sad, polite and detached, this decently bred and educated man spent his days moving about discreetly between his wigs and his properties. He drank with the intensity of such Russian characters, or of Irish tinkers attending a succession of fair days. With wigs he was a genius—his pride alone surpassed his skill. He would not receive an individual tip from anyone; discretion had to be used, taking the form of a collection handed to him as a present at the end of the season—when he had little else but this gift to live on during the annual holidays. He read extensively the Russian classics out of the Company's travelling library. He always travelled in solitary splendour, for he was never known to take a bath, wash his hair, or get his suit cleaned, so that he would find himself (however crowded the travelling arrangements) with an entire carriage at his disposal, where he could lie down and go to sleep in comfort. Experience had taught his companions on the staff that a crowded carriage was by far the lesser of two evils. . . .

Only once did a drinking bout inflame his imagination and cause him to cast care aside. The Company arrived at the theatre one evening to find all the eighteenth-century wigs for *Aurora's Wedding* fantastically dressed as birds, ships and any other work of fantasy that the wigmaker's skilled fingers could conjure up.

Rumour says that years later he was found dead by, or in, a Paris sewer: the Dostoievsky character had had a fitting end.

This Russian *émigré* ballet company appeared to me a group of artists that a puff of wind might blow to all corners of the earth. They lived intensely and worked very hard. In their presence I would feel guilty of possessing too many of the world's goods; I found it unwise to contemplate the future of some of them, for the picture was already outlined in all its fatalistic hopelessness: many seemed mortal beings engulfed in a whirlwind that was not of their seeking.

Their private parties always left me sad. Held in various corners of Europe, in celebration of some calendar date, or as a means to grow momentarily closer in this wandering life, things would start quietly enough. There would be vodka, caviar and Russian folk songs, Russian toasts and Russian jokes; then would come the moment for those to depart who did not want to be present at a crazy dawn, when it was inevitable that one would witness a temporarily broken friendship or two. To my relief, these artists, with their intelligence and sensitivity, made it clear that they thought far less of you if you stayed on: for to stay and remain sober was merely vulgar curiosity: you gave no offence by removing yourself at the correct time.

I never saw the last hours of a company party; nor did two-thirds of my companions.

•   •   •

But in the end (my end only) I discovered that I did not really belong; only gratitude for a vast collection of unselected and undigested knowledge remained. Mentally, more than physically, one longed to get away, for I felt stifled and restricted.

Artists are sometimes surprised when I regard such an expression of feeling on their part with sympathy. It is like that, though, with some of us; we must have change. It is surely my duty, when confronted with these particular circumstances, to remember my own youth, and my revolt against the intimate life of the great rehearsal-room and dressing-room, the only variation to which consisted of long train journeys, where we were more closely packed together than ever. But for those that it suits, a theatre community life can hold much of light and shade, of infinite interest and variety.

When I left Diaghilev the question of the classical ballet still worried me; how much it worried me is clear to me now. In retrospect, I note that I made a gesture of complete subjection: I applied for an engagement with the Pavlova Company. Only after my interview with her manager, Dandré, at which I discussed details of my engagement, I was stopped in my plan by a feeling of guilt towards Diaghilev.

In relation to the Pavlova project, I shall always regret that I considered anything beyond the carrying out of my first inclination; that instinct was right; one year along such specialized lines would have been highly beneficial to me. I had wanted to get back to pure dancing for one year, prior to taking up teaching, as an aid to further study from the instructor's angle. The Russian teachers in Paris, with whom I had so often studied, had inspired this feeling.

I have often regretted the opportunity that I missed of working at close quarters with Anna Pavlova.

The main effect of Diaghilev on my dormant creative mind was to arouse an intense interest in the ballet in relation to the theatre. I further sensed its own singular position in the theatre; this in spite of the fact that many of the later ballets (that were produced when I was with the Company) struck me as of little importance.

I had come to one conclusion: the same should happen, along the same lines, and with just such an ultimate goal—in England.

I wanted to see this achieved with the same passionate feeling of dedication that a little girl once felt about dancing an Irish jig to music. Over twenty years ago a child had once sensed the difference between an exhibition of fancy dancing and an authentic National dance; as a young artist, the former child now sensed the dignity of the dance in the theatre as an art form in unity with many things.

* * *

The saga of the Russian Ballet forms a pattern in my life: I will show the pattern complete to the inclusion of one small thread, bridging a period of forty-six years.

In 1956 I was invited to view the traditional Russian Ballet at close quarters; the roots that I so vaguely and mysteriously felt behind that organization which Diaghilev had ruled with such autocratic yet eclectic domination.

It is a day in February and I am sitting in the Bolshoi Theatre in Moscow; it is twelve noon, and I am about to witness a midday performance of *Le Lac des Cygnes*. Thirty years have passed over my head since I dreamt of an English National Ballet; thirty years have culminated in my presence in the historical Russian theatre, on a visit made with the express purpose of discussing the prospect of two National ballet Companies making a cultural exchange.

The older School had already inspired England for many years through the offspring that had for so long resided on foreign soil; now in the Bolshoi theatre sits an English dancer who had benefited by a close contact with the branch that had left its native land some forty years ago.

In the great gold and white theatre my eyes travel round the tiers of boxes—packed to the utmost as is every other part of the building. This theatre is an immense state organization, with an imposing proportion of the whole dedicated to the dance.

Just as the Bolshoi artists were born to this rich heritage, so was the audience born to share in the same heritage as part of their cultural education; a similar historic process is evolving in England very much along these lines.

Outside the snow falls: as it falls it freezes and is then chipped off the pavements with heavy spades. At the side of the roads and pavements great mounds of snow, several feet high, resemble white glistening hedges. But inside the theatre and again inside the school, (with its lofty rooms equipped with perfect central heating), gossamer-clad figures dance, and I witness at close range the legendary Russian Ballet at work.

The leisure that I had once felt in the Abbey Theatre I feel again here, but there is a fundamental difference: in Dublin everything had seemed personal and individual, in Moscow the atmosphere strikes me as impersonal and collective.

The Russian artists speak earnestly of contact with the West, and I found that our dancers and ballets are well known by name. It is the Sadler's Wells Ballet that represents the ballet of Western Europe for these Russian artists.

Would we take with us, on our visit to Moscow, the works of Fokine? Would we please present Stravinsky's *L'Oiseau de Feu*?

In the year 1911 a little girl sat in a box at Covent Garden Opera House. She was watching, for the first time in her life, Karsavina dance: the ballets presented included *L'Oiseau de Feu*. In the year 1956 this little girl (who has so long outgrown that shantung silk party dress and her best silk mittens) is in Moscow, and she is attending a conference of Russian theatre dignitaries. . . .

Among the many matters discussed she is assuring them that the English National Ballet will most certainly bring *L'Oiseau de Feu* back to its native Russia in the late autumn of 1956.

Thus it is that history sometimes goes into reverse.

IV

BOTH SIDES OF THE RIVER

... 'The life of a person or a part,' explained the Director, 'consists of an unending change of objects; circles of attention, either on the plane of reality or of the imagination in the realm of memories of the past or dreams about the future. The unbroken quality of this line is of the utmost importance to an artist, and you should learn to establish it in yourself . . .'

CONSTANTIN STANISLAVSKY, *An Actor Prepares*

IN THE summer of 1926 I opened a private school in a studio in Roland Gardens, Gloucester Road. I had left the Diaghilev Ballet about ten months previously, although I still appeared with them occasionally in London. That very summer I was with them at His Majesty's Theatre.

I was anxious to take up production work, and decided that the repertory theatre movement throughout the country would not only prove to be the best possible form of production experience for me, but might also be the only theatrical venture that would show any interest in the foundation of a repertory ballet company.

That autumn my cousin, Terence Gray, was to open the Festival Theatre at Cambridge, and he invited me to join the staff as choreographer. I had also managed to obtain an introduction to Lilian Baylis of the Old Vic.

The following years were to drive me to and fro over the Thames via Waterloo Bridge, and to and fro from London to Cambridge, sometimes stretched out in a third class carriage on the milk train after a first night, so as to get to my school early in the morning. By 1928 Dublin had joined in the fun, and I would find myself bobbing like a cork on the Liverpool night mailboat on my way to the Abbey Theatre.

How do I look back on those years? With affection and a very real nostalgia; one was young and full of energy and fired with an optimism that was sustained by as passionate a love of the theatre as the good clown has for the ring.

The furthest hills are greenest . . . and in retrospect some of the
hills that I have climbed and left behind me are still the fairest and
greenest of all, for their paths led as far as I dared my dreams to go
ahead of me.

Sometimes I think that I planned everything. But does one ever
really plan? It was no plan that taught a small girl an Irish Jig on a
cottage stone floor . . . it was some force at work—of which neither
she nor others had any knowledge.

It was during that early summer of 1926, with its disturbing
General Strike, its fair weather and my personal optimism, on one of
those fine mornings that I donned the best of my summer wardrobe
and, in a huge floppy hat, went to see Lilian Baylis.

Now time and events must wait awhile; for that fine morning
when I first crossed Waterloo Bridge to visit the South side was the
most important bit of bridge-crossing that I had ever undertaken,
repercussions of which are to be felt to this day. I must therefore
first recall Miss Lilian Baylis, who was to be known to me for the
next eleven years as 'The Lady'.

·   ·   ·

Strange is the weaving of the pattern, for Lilian Baylis was a pupil
of a Wordsworth head teacher. One of Miss Baylis's early missions
was to preach a little of the gospel of 'fancy dancing' on the Rand.

Her history has been brilliantly recorded by far more skilful pens
than mine. There is only left for me, as a member of her staff, to tell
of the impact of her personality.

I arrived at the Old Vic on a Saturday—I suppose it must have been
late in May. There was a matinée performance, I think, of *The
Taming of the Shrew*, and it was the season when Dame Edith Evans
was sweeping all before her.

Evelyn Williams, 'The Lady's' private secretary, was also present;
I was nervous, yet determined to stand my ground and get as good a
hearing as possible for my plans: the formation of a British Ballet
through the good offices of the Old Vic.

Looking back on it today, I cannot conceive why I struck 'The Lady' as anything more than a slightly fanatical young woman.

At the end of my peroration concerning the possibilities of a British Ballet, she informed me that she liked my face; she then added that she thought I was practical and appeared to have had a great deal of professional experience. She next went on to tell me that she had no money and no second theatre as yet; there were no rehearsal rooms and there was nothing to be done.

My heart sank so low that only dimly did I hear the sequel; a sequel that showed that the pill had a thin coating of sugar.

She was looking, so the voice informed my dizzy senses, for some-one to teach the drama students how to move. She said that they all had dreadful hands, and that most actors and actresses had dreadful hands, and as they did not know what to do with their hands, they appeared in the end to be even more dreadful; she added that she preferred beautiful hands to beautiful faces.

Having disposed of all hands belonging to the dramatic profession, she then fingered some letters on her desk and told me they were from people after the job that she was going to offer to me; she was offering it to me because she was now convinced that I knew more than all the other applicants—although one was even recommended by Sybil Thorndike, but dear Sybil had a way sometimes of recom-mending people just out of the kindness of her heart. . . .

She then came back to the sugared pill; she was looking for some-one to arrange any little dance required in the Shakespearian pro-ductions; she wanted someone to give a look to her office workers, who obliged by appearing in a voluntary capacity in the opera ballets; she would like a short (expenses only) ballet performance put on at Christmas before *Hansel and Gretel* by some good ballet school, and a lot more angels from the same source for the Opera itself.

She thought that I had by far the highest qualifications to take on all this, but she did not expect all my work to be voluntary; I would receive £1 per week for teaching the dramatic students and £2 for arranging any choreography required in a Shakespeare production.

In addition, I would lead a host of 'expenses only' dancers in the Christmas Ballet production, and supervise the voluntary Opera Ballet office workers, and guarantee student angels galore for *Hansel and Gretel*.

I then visited her voluntary Opera *corps de ballet*. One girl had a wooden hand, but Miss Baylis informed me that an excellent kid glove was preserved for her special use. I decided there and then that this particular work should be given to a senior student from my school, who must, in return, receive a small pittance for her labour. Young Rosalind Iden, at that time a student of mine, most gallantly carried out the work of the Opera Ballet.

Thus, briefly, did Lilian Baylis contract me to the services of the Old Vic for four years, ever dangling in front of my eyes the rebuilding of Sadler's Wells in the dim future. I earned, on the average, about £40 per annum.

Lilian Baylis has been sketched by many; stories about her are legion, and I have no wish to join the ranks of those who succeed only in stressing her as a quaint character. In my opinion this is to underestimate her wholly. Above all, she was a very real person, and it was from this quality that she derived her strength of purpose. Mentally, she was not unlike a sincere, shrewd, devout peasant. She sprang from those decades of the Victorian age that were preoccupied with reform, and the first person to influence her in this direction was her aunt—Emma Cons. This aunt owned property in the Waterloo Road, and was much concerned with the moral standards of the Old Vic which was on her property. She set out to reform matters there.

People have called Miss Baylis mean, but I emphatically refute this accusation. She thought about money as a peasant thinks about it— safer in the stocking than in the bank. She thought that banks were clever robbers, and regarded with suspicion business transactions concerned with 'loans'. She considered any debt as a matter of honour

LENNOX ROBINSON

WILLIAM BUTLER YEATS AT 'SORRENTO' DALKEY
(*Lennox Robinson's Cottage*)

Peter McCormack

OLIVER ST. JOHN GOGARTY'S GARDEN PARTY DURING AONACH TAILTEANN, 1923

Front row, left to right: W. B. Yeats, Compton Mackenzie, Augustus John, Sir Edwin Lutyens

Back row, left to right: G. K. Chesterton, James Stephens, Lennox Robinson

eventually requiring honourable discharge; but she could not see, if your intentions were honourable, why you should be robbed (her views on interest) during your struggle to repay.

She had, however, strong views on discount as a fitting reward for prompt payment. For money down (even on a modest account), I have heard her demand five per cent discount—a healthy enough challenge to all hire purchase systems, and perhaps an unconscious effort on the part of Miss Baylis to get even with the banks.

Her morality was of the old school, tempered with the true reformer's rather robust philosophy concerning the fallen; she was far too human to patronize or condemn and an emergency found her practical, helpful and cheerful. She said that 'nature' was so beautiful, so simple; but when Miss Baylis spoke of 'nature' she meant, in the language of today, the facts of life. She loved, she said, all the boys and girls around her to be happy, and liked everything to be beautifully natural, until in fact that really was the case. I well recall being summoned to discuss a noticeable romance between two artists. I listened politely to a tale of woe and worry over two adult persons in her theatre and gravely promised to look into things. But the old lady was not hoodwinked. When I left the office she informed her secretary that I was not really shocked; no doubt I had been too long in the Russian Ballet . . .

The body beautiful was her great topic; on this point she had no inhibitions. I once stood with her at the back of the Old Vic circle during a ballet performance when she informed me, in clear loud tones, that a certain male dancer had a most beautiful behind.

She would take great exception to incidents in plays or ballets which she considered ignored beauty. I was not spoken to once for some days, because of a ballet I produced in which a baby was stung to death by a mischievous scorpion. It mattered not that the Goddess Iris hastily restored the baby, alive, to its mother: Miss Baylis thought the incident horrible and due, in all probability, to the fact that I obviously had no maternal instinct. Another time she considered that, on the backcloth of 'Rio Grande', Edward Burra had distorted the body beautiful of a female statue: when we returned

7

from lunch it was discovered that she had had the offending nude painted out.

It always distresses me to hear anyone debunk her religion. She was a truly devout woman; it was her direct simple thinking that mixed the material and the spiritual in her statements. Her approach was not unlike the negro conception of religion as expressed in negro spirituals. The old story of 'Sorry, dear, God says No', to the wretched actor who asked for a ten shilling rise in his weekly salary, meant that Miss Baylis's conscience—aware of overdrafts, voluntary workers and others in the same financial plight—prompted her not to be persuaded by anyone; in such circumstances she would ask for guidance and be convinced she had received it.

Of course, over the years, she had to make big breaks with many of her major principles. After an obstinate fight, she would eventually take the hurdle in a truly feminine fashion, landing on the other side with a clear conscience. She would be comfortably aware that she had been beaten in a straight fight, and not unaware that she was relieved to give up the struggle over an embarrassing and impractical principle.

The end of temperance at the Old Vic and Sadler's Wells finally came about, and showed the Lady to be a gallant loser. When the Wells was rebuilt it was decided that the audience could not, in the year 1931, be deprived of a bar. Once Miss Baylis had recovered from the disloyalty to Aunt Emma, to the coffee house tradition, and to the triumphant overthrow of gin palaces in the past, she decided on a large-scale campaign to reinstate gin as a financial aid to culture, carrying her capitulation to a shrewd and unexpected extreme.

Sadler's Wells Theatre was to be the first and only theatre to have a bar on both sides of the proscenium. If, for the good of the theatre's finances and the comfort of the patrons, drink was to be served on the premises, Miss Baylis decided that the stage staff, artists and orchestral players should not waste their wages supporting the local public house; they could hand some of their pay back to the theatre by means of a bar backstage. She felt, no doubt, that even

Aunt Emma would have found such capitulation practical. In the case of the orchestra the arrangement was a particularly happy one; orchestras were so very expensive.

The Lady would genuinely panic over money. It became an obsession with her, but one that rightly demanded everyone's sympathy because she was rarely without a certain amount of financial worry. She developed a habit of asking for £1,000 because, as she said, one way and another she always seemed to be losing that exact amount of money. Standing on the stage with me one night after a comparatively lucrative season, she asked me what she should say. I told her to say anything she liked but not to ask for money . . . she threw me a look of sheer agony and gasped, 'My dear, I must . . .'

One matinée, I came off the Old Vic stage where I had just danced *Spectre de la Rose* with Dolin. I had an urgent message to go to Miss Baylis at once. I found her sitting at her desk, with the box office returns in her hands. The command was: 'Sit down, dear,' and wearily I sank into a chair, still clad in poke bonnet and crinoline. 'We are losing money on these matinées. What are you going to do about it, dear?' For one fleeting moment the inopportunity of asking a breathless Victorian maiden to consider financial matters must have flashed across my face, for I was told not to worry, but instead, to have a cup of tea.

If I had to mention anything that I found really irritating about her, it would be her dogs, long tangle-haired creatures that left you wondering which end you were patting.

Always in the office and always in the way, they spent their time charging at their owner in an effort to get on to her lap, rattling in their progress the inevitable teacup, breaking up any sequence of conversation with yelps that made me long to throttle them. I suffered their presence year in and year out. She would wander round the theatre carrying these shapeless O–Cedar mops, one under each arm. If she wished to point out any feature of interest a dog was dropped; it would land, yelping, on your feet, successfully drowning the observation that led to its downfall.

There was a day when (with dog under each arm) she watched a nervous young actor endeavouring to get through a difficult rôle at short notice. Miss Baylis at last charged down the centre aisle: 'Thank you, dear. It won't do, dear, you are not very good, are you, dear?' With the final 'are you, dear?' both dogs flopped to the floor only to scurry under the seats, for once silenced and abashed by 'The Lady's' disconcerting directness.

'The Lady' always expected everyone to show what she ruthlessly termed 'guts'. Guts amounted to producing a tired poker face in adversity, leaving Miss Baylis to do the guessing.

She could not bear anyone to become hysterical at the sight of trouble. She once told a distracted, pregnant unmarried young woman (whom she had befriended to the point of getting the young man to the altar and paying for the wedding herself) that if she didn't pull herself together the baby would be born before she got to the church. This gloomy prophecy worked with a curative speed that would have been the envy of any doctor.

She inspired affection and loyalty from those who worked with her. She informed me once that she was very ignorant, but she always knew who knew. What she did not know, in her great and fearless simplicity, was that she possessed something greater than knowledge —a natural wisdom; this wisdom sprang from experience, piety and kindliness, the paths that lead to human understanding.

Her house in Brixton stood still in time. It would be crowded to the roof once every year when she welcomed half London's theatre world to her pre-season reception. With its stuffy rooms choked with bric-à-brac, its ornate garden furnishings, this comfortable middle-class home was typical of London's gaslit nineteenth-century suburbia.

The last time that I saw her concluded for me a cycle in time.

The first production that I ever did for Miss Baylis (in 1926) was the choreography for *A Midsummer Night's Dream*, and by a strange turn of the wheel, this play was again in rehearsal on a certain November morning in 1937.

That day I found her tired and a little despondent. We discussed the possibility of staging *The Sleeping Beauty* for the following autumn, a long-cherished wish that it had at last become possible to fulfil, thanks to the new wardrobe space that had been allowed for at Sadler's Wells. She spoke of retirement; she said that she felt the ballet was safe in my hands and the drama in Guthrie's, but she was worried as to who would take charge of the opera.

The office door was open; this never bothered 'The Lady', but I always found it disconcerting and so I asked whether I might close it. We discussed the matter for some minutes, for she expressed surprise at my odd wish for seclusion, typified in her mind by a closed office door.

The interview was similar to many others that had taken place over the years of our work together. The same sights and sounds: the dogs scampered as usual, the tea was on the desk, as was also the little framed picture of Dürer's Praying Hands.

I could also see 'The Lady's' own fine hands; they seemed as expressive, expansive and capable as usual. Perhaps though they alone defied the tired face, the heavy slumped body, and the slightly hesitant mind.

* * *

She died peacefully, forty-eight hours later. Evelyn Williams rang me very early on that morning and simply said, ' "The Lady" is dead.'

Thus quietly do great influences pass from our lives.

* * *

I am back now in 1926 and it is the autumn of my first season as a staff member of the Vic-Wells organization, to which I have belonged—without a break—until this day.

My Vic drama students had awkward hands, and their hands were matched by equally awkward feet. Developing a system of movement for them was my first task, my second was to keep them interested.

I had Elizabeth Allan in the class. She was very pretty, but she frightened me considerably as she had cartilage trouble in one knee. I can see her sitting on the floor, crying with pain, one bad day when the cartilage slipped during her dancing lesson. Heather Angel, another student, was then a small girl with a long straight fringe; later she was to make a film name for herself in America. There stands out firmly, however, my favourite and most painstaking pupil—Esmond Knight. He would have made a wonderful dancer, as he possessed quite the most remarkable jump that I have ever seen.

It was the season with Jean Forbes-Robertson—young and so beautiful, and with so much promise. Her first rôle was Juliet. I saw a great deal of her rehearsals, as I had to arrange the ballroom scene dance. She had a beautiful voice and a strange ethereal personality; I found her balcony scene deeply moving.

I embarked on a fair amount of choreography for the autumn production of *A Midsummer Night's Dream*—using the drama students for the fairy scenes. With my own students, and the help of Ursula Moreton, Hedley Briggs and Stanley Judson, I staged a short ballet to go before *Hansel and Gretel* at Christmas. Every winter a small ballet was staged as a curtain raiser.

My private school continued, and my students danced at the Old Vic or were carted up to Cambridge once or twice a term to take part in a Greek chorus or give a week of short ballet performances. Sometimes two or three of them would go to Dublin with me to perform in a week of dancing at the Abbey Theatre when two little ballets might be given with one of Yeats's *Plays for Dancers*.

During these years I taught once every week at Heathfield School at Ascot. Half-hour classes ran right through the afternoon. One very pretty but particularly naughty small girl reduced me one day to exasperation. I demanded her name and was informed it was Alexandra. 'Alexandra what?' I snapped. 'Alexandra of Greece,' was the answer. 'Alexandra of Greece' was sent to sit down. Thus I can record that I once put the future consort of the King of Yugoslavia in the corner.

The Festival Theatre opened in the autumn of 1926. The first production was *The Orestia*, for which I supplied a chorus made up of students, and also arranged the choreography. It was an exciting production; the new theatre, with its apron stage ending in a flight of steps, was considered the last thing in modernity.

I can remember one day Professor Robert Trevelyan standing with me in the stalls—it was his translation of the play that we were using. As with all authors, his nose was buried in the book; he was concerned only with keeping a careful check on the words of the actors. It was the opening scene with the herald. He sighed, and reminded me that a production of the play in the summer of 1914 had been staged by the Cambridge Dramatic Society and that for that performance his herald had been Rupert Brooke. An unknown young actor was playing Orestes for us; it was his first engagement and he had come straight from one of Cramer's piano shops; his name was Maurice Evans.

The Festival Theatre was an exhilarating place to work in, but the venture met with a mixed reception from the town, which was divided sharply for and against. Terence Gray delighted in upsetting those who were prepared to be upset, but he did a great deal to make Cambridge conscious and proud of its first professional repertory theatre. He ran the theatre for five years and lost a great deal of money, but a number of distinguished people in the theatre today trod those boards during his directorship, and I do not think that any of us who worked there remember the venture as anything but a happy one.

Cambridge in the spring and autumn; this charming theatre situated just outside the main part of the town on the Newmarket Road . . . it remains one of my green hills that has not faded with time and change: the Greek plays, the Restoration comedies, and

Dekker's *Shoemaker's Holiday*, with Boris Ord at the harpsichord . . . the enchanting poet Gordon Bottomley and his delight with the choreography that I arranged for W. B. Yeats's *On Baile's Strand*.

Meanwhile the Abbey Theatre suddenly twined in and out of the busy life I led, a life which, for five years, was two-thirds dedicated to the wants and wishes of poets, authors, producers, actors and actresses. . . .

•   •   •

It is the year 1927 and I am sitting in the dark vestibule of the Festival Theatre in Cambridge. I am listening to a rich Irish voice that seems to intone a request that I should come to Dublin and produce for the Abbey Theatre. The voice belongs to William Butler Yeats, who has just witnessed a verse play of Gordon Bottomley's and some dance creations of my own. . . . It would seem that if I should return to Ireland at his impressive bidding (made to me in a light so dim that the speaker's features were not clear) I would work among those people whose efforts to establish the Irish Theatre were in progress at the time that I struggled with an Irish Jig in a farmhouse at the foot of the Wicklow Hills.

The mind of Yeats was made up; he would have a small school of Ballet at the Abbey and I would send over a teacher. I would visit Dublin every three months and produce his *Plays for Dancers* and perform in them myself; thus, he said, the poetic drama of Ireland would live again and take its rightful place in the Nation's own Theatre, and the oblivion imposed on it by the popularity of peasant drama would become a thing of the past.

'W.B.' carried the day with his distinguished directors, Lady Gregory, Dr. Walter Starkie and Lennox Robinson. I found myself in Dublin with a dancer who had been a student of mine (Vivienne Bennett, the actress) and the small school was opened. I then decided on some small productions that we should be able to present six months later, as Miss Bennett was only able to stay for that length of time; her place was then taken by Sara Payne, the sister of Rosalind Iden.

The work at the Abbey had much of interest. A number of Yeats's *Plays for Dancers* were given, two or three new works in verse, and several short Irish ballets suitable for young dancers.

In 1916 Yeats had written the following notes on *The Hawk's Well*:

... Perhaps I shall turn to something else now that our Japanese dancer, Mr. Itow, whose minute intensity of movement in the dance of the hawk so well suited our small room and private art, has been hired by a New York theatre, or perhaps I shall find another dancer. ...

In the late twenties, W. B. Yeats found another dancer for *The Hawk's Well*, for I danced this rôle myself. I was the first to achieve this distinction after Mr. Itow—and I even succeeded in wearing his costume. Yeats re-wrote *The King of the Great Clock Tower* and *The Only Jealousy of Emer* so that the 'Queen' in the former and the 'Woman of the Sidhe' in the latter could be interpreted by me in dance mime, wearing masks for both rôles.

The Abbey Theatre in the mid-twenties was at the height of its international fame and had the distinction of being the only national theatre in our midst. The first company of players (which included Sara and Maire O'Neil, Florence Farr, Arthur Sinclair and the Fay Brothers) had broken away from the Abbey and were scattered mainly between the theatres of London and New York. In my time, the Abbey's production director was Lennox Robinson and the second company consisted of such distinguished Abbey-trained artists as Barry Fitzgerald, Maureen Delaney, Peter McCormack, Eileen Crowe, Sheila Richards, Arthur Shields and Michael Dolan. They shouldered brilliantly the tradition laid down by their predecessors.

The Irish are natural actors. They have a great sense of timing and interplay. Their voices are rich in feeling and they stress with ease the music that is to be found in words of common speech; they can all intone; with them the 'keen' becomes a strange chant within the range of any group of Irish players.

By the nature of its economic structure, life in the Abbey Theatre was a pleasant, leisurely affair, wearing an air of semi-professionalism. Most of the male actors had a further means of livelihood, in fact the full-time company of players represented quite a small part of the whole. How well these players knew their repertoire! They wore it with the affection and familiarity of old and comfortable clothes, growing into many of their characters and seeming to live them in life—both in gesture and intonation.

The famous green room, hung with framed copies of Yeats's early poems, was furnished with comfortable chairs, a coal fire burnt when necessary and there would always be a pot of tea brewing. This room might so resemble the parlour scene just enacted on the stage that to join the players in the interval was to make one feel that we were all continuing with the play. Conversation was parlour conversation, but eyes would light up if anyone mentioned America. I have seen Maureen Delaney roll her eyes to the click of her knitting needles at the recollection of the blissful speakeasies, for some of the last tours were at the height of the prohibition.

The National Theatre lived through many stormy times; most of its directors were Protestant and I think that in the early and difficult years this may well have added to the misunderstanding and confusion—absurd in fact, for never were a body of people at heart more in sympathy with the Irish as a race and with Ireland as a country apart. But the attitude of these cultured people towards the national self-expression in the theatre was a hundred years in advance of either Catholic or Protestant in the Ireland of that day. Only isolated members of the Anglo-Irish showed any interest in the national theatre movement; even as late as 1928, I heard it said that the trouble with the Abbey was that it was built on the wrong side of the river. Thus, at the beginning, a group of tolerant and idealistic poets and writers were misunderstood all round. Their idealism was hampered by lack of money and a naturally amateur approach to practical problems; but the saddest aspect was the lethargy of the country-house dwellers and the antagonism of the priests and half their flock, not to mention the inflammable political situation. Eventually the money that they needed to give the venture the mildest form of security came from Miss Horniman, the woman who had already founded one famous repertory theatre—the Gaiety in Manchester.

The Abbey was unique. I hate to think of the green room and the tiny row of dressing-rooms resembling narrow log cabins gone for ever. It was the unostentatious back street setting that lent this theatre its individuality. Horse Show week would bring flocks of American visitors searching out the home of the famed Irish Players who toured the States from coast to coast. The small entrance hall was decorated with playbills from foreign countries and woolly oil paintings by Jack Yeats of players and playwrights; in the theatre's auditorium, there was that little miscalculation on the part of the architect which resulted in the dress circle being most rakishly off-centre.

Many are the stories that I heard of the early days. Yeats was supposed to have engaged Lennox Robinson as manager in obedience to the promptings of his Celtic voices, for he announced one day that the post must be offered to a young man sitting in front of him in the theatre, because of the shape of his head. Unless my memory is at fault, it was the poet himself who told me of his determination in this matter. Then there is another lively story from the same source. In the early days a certain distinguished player, perhaps bored with her own distinction, announced that she wanted to produce a play. This request is not unusual from those whose creative talents are non-existent. It goes with a frustration that is based on a wish to express authority; it is the authority associated with the work of the producer that is the real source of the ambition. The directors decided to let her have her way. On the day of the first rehearsal Yeats and Lennox Robinson sat in the stalls. The play started and the lady, seated at last in the middle of the stalls, in her position of solitary splendour, said nothing. Yeats, resolutely overflowing with the milk of human kindness, felt that she might indeed be nervous, and so he would slip away altogether for a short time, but Lennox would only seem to slip away; in reality the latter was to return immediately and seek obscurity at the back of the pit. After a lapse of time, Yeats crept back to join the other in the pit and to inquire after production progress. 'She hasn't said anything, and the play is well on,' said Lennox. Undaunted, Yeats announced that it was quite possible that she might still be feeling their presence, and so they would make quite a show of going out together; Lennox would then creep upstairs and peep at proceedings from the darkest corner in the circle. Some time later Yeats joined him again. The back of the static silent female form was still visible; it appeared to be disconcertingly unscathed by the agile progress of the play, which was travelling forward with the speed of a driverless ghost train. 'Nothing has been said at all, and the play is near the end,' said Lennox.

Time, at the Abbey, of course, stood still for the general convenience of everyone. Productions were carried through in an atmosphere of leisurely Celtic twilight. I can recall the flautist who so beautifully rehearsed with us for *The Hawk's Well*. When the rehearsal was finished he remembered that the days chosen for the performances would be out of the question . . . they were too inconvenient . . . he had not understood. . . . Faintly was his announcement relayed through the dark empty theatre with more curiosity than consternation; like an echo was the statement handed on, everyone hoping that someone had broad enough shoulders to accept the final impact. A gentle half-sigh eventually dismissed the matter and the waste of time was generously written off; it was not the kind of waste that would bother a hair of the head of anyone born in Dublin.

It is always the unexpected that the Irishman expects of life; yet when it happens to him at home the effect is often sterile, for many an Irishman on his native soil seems to start the business of dying on the day that he is born. If, however, the unexpected should hit him as an emigrant on foreign soil, he shows every ingenuity, turns it to good account and thrives on it. The average Irishman can do half a dozen things and he can do them well—provided that he can pick his fancy. I am reminded of Barney, the Abbey theatre cleaner of those days, a gentle, silent, beautiful old man who, with a sad sense of care, carried out his cleaning duties by day. How would it be to find an English theatre cleaner installed in the prompt corner? Yet, Barney would be prompter with a range of plays from Shaw to Yeats's *Plays for Dancers*.

I would sometimes hear further stories of those hearty days when the theatre would incense its fiery audience to the point of giving them a pretext for a riot. Proudly Yeats informed me that O'Casey's *The Plough and the Stars* inspired three riots in various prominent parts of Dublin. Dr. Larchet, the musical director, would describe happenings inside the theatre. There was a performance of the play, he said, when they came over the footlights like waves; their indignation was such and their sense of propriety and politics so confused that, with the excitement of it all, they wrapped in a rug a theatrically consumptive girl attired in a theatrical nightdress before they thought it fit to bundle her off and out into the street with the rest of the cast!

My days were more quiet; but even then there was a charming Dublin priest, who could not attend performances, and so was present at all full dress rehearsals . . . and the old members of the pit would still obligingly prompt an actor suffering from a sudden loss of a word. There was the old suspicion accorded to poetic drama—and a deadly resentful silence would settle on the theatre's old-timers like a sulky fog. One night, a Yeats's play containing a line to the effect that a man grows tired of his wife resulted in penetration of the sulky fog; a fog-horn of a human voice announced 'that's bloody true!'

•　　　•　　　•

In the twenties when Dr. Gogarty was walking down Grafton Street he was also holding his fortnightly salons. I can see his drawing-room filled with the Yeats family, the Walter Starkies, the Lennox Robinsons, the John McCormacks, James Stephens, 'Æ' (George Russel) and the rest of Dublin's intelligentsia. I only met Æ once; yet I can still see that Celtic mystic reclining in an armchair with his hands outspread and the tips of his fingers meeting, forming an arch over his chest. Has anyone described him with greater sincerity of feeling than George Moore? . . . 'The reason why I have not included any personal description of Æ is because he exists rather in one's imagination, dreams, sentiments, feelings, than in one's ordinary sight and hearing, and try as I will to catch the fleeting outlines they escape me; and all I remember are the long pantheistic eyes that have looked so often into my soul with such a kindly gaze . . .'

Dr. Gogarty would tell his stories and there would sometimes be mild cracks at America, mainly by those who had been there on lecture tours and felt that something of the sort was expected of them. One evening John McCormack (a staunch supporter of the New World) considered that the jokes had gone too far; his burst of irritation was followed by a shy silence, dispersed by Gogarty, who told of an old lady that he once knew who would end all moments of embarrassment by questioning the world at large as to which they would rather be eaten by—an alligator or a crocodile. . . .

•   •   •

With affection and esteem will I always see two figures—Lennox Robinson, a long quiet untidy-looking eagle, peering at us from the gloom of the Abbey stalls with his glasses reflecting shafts of light; occasionally his look would stray to the book held between the long tapering fingers. Close to him there would be Yeats with his pince-nez dangerously near the end of his nose. This pince-nez was tied to a long flowing black ribbon attaching itself to some obscure point in the voluminous cape—a cape which seemed to hold the great figure loosely together, turning it into a vague monumental shape. He would appear to me as a heroic legendary figure—a Cuchullain fighting more than the waves: for Yeats fought prejudice with passion, ignorance with irony, criticism with humility. The fighter in him showed a man with a passionate sense of justice and a curious practical streak. He was, though, an aristocrat at heart; his reasons were not based on sentiment, they were essentially practical. He told me that artists could only give of their best if the world permitted them the patronage of a leisured aristocracy. He maintained that the common mass of humanity was too concerned with the business of living: they had not the time at their disposal to make those singular demands for perfection which should be asked of the artist.

It has been said that Yeats was vain, and that he lacked humour. It struck me that his moments of vanity belonged to the modest variety that all artists acquire; their capacity of self-valuation is sharpened, as a result of intense self-criticism; their appreciation of any praise bestowed on them springs from the feeling that they have achieved a positive expression of their creative ideas. His views on life were tempered with a sensitive approach to the human side of earthly existence; on occasions this brought his reactions, in their lively imaginings, near enough to something more expressive of humour than scholarly wit.

Conversation with Yeats could be likened to a verbal switchback: up and down it would go, and then a corner would be taken at full speed, a long slow climb, a breath-taking dive, only to find that the impetus had carried you once more to the heights. He told me that at the beginning of the Irish Literary Theatre movement his friends would ask him what he was going to do about keeping trained actors in Dublin; his answer was that he was not going to do anything as the Dublin accent would do it for him. Then again it would be all talk of dreams and visions and he would affirm to me that all the greatest excitements of his life had taken place in his head. He could start a conversation with the announcement that the previous night he had had a vision, in a tone of voice usually bestowed on the remembrance of a round of golf. His relaxation was the reading of detective stories. Mrs. Yeats, discovered in a faintly harassed frame of mind in Grafton Street, informed me that Willie was leaving for Cork and she had to find him a detective story for the train journey. I remarked that it should be easy enough, but Mrs. Yeats said that it was not so easy as the book must have a love interest.

Someone should write a book to commemorate the wives of poets and artists. With their feet firmly planted on the ground and their heads concentrated on showing every ounce of feminine adaptability to the clouds, they dexterously weave their way through a maze of poetic turmoil and contradiction; they are patient, solid and practical, arriving at the end of an argument long before anyone else present; I have often compared their private solutions to post office savings, not to be drawn out without due notice.

I can remember a certain turmoil between Yeats and Dulac and the shock it was to the decorum of the B.B.C.; the eventual disentanglement was the result of months of a feminine underground movement on the part of two devoted wives, brightly aware of male childishness. Yeats had been once more trying to broadcast an example of Irish poetic drama set to music by Dulac . . . the poet was upset over the English rendering of the songs, Dulac elated. Yeats expounded how such a rendering would make it impossible for him to face his Dublin friends again, so ashamed he was at the let-down to them all. The musical but fiery Frenchman, with quite different views as to who must not be let down, informed Yeats that he must, if necessary, offend Dublin, as he happened to be for the moment in a civilized country. The dignified pale young men of the B.B.C. went several shades paler and Yeats stalked out. The broadcast was highly successful; two wives worked in mutual accord for several months to heal the wound inflicted.

The digression is over; we are back in the darkened theatre with Lennox Robinson and Yeats. Catching himself up in every form of seat and arm-rest, Yeats moves towards Lennox, for he would ask his old friend if he had any idea what he meant when he wrote the line that the actor has just declaimed. Maybe the line was almost the age of Lennox himself. But no matter. That understanding creature would always know something, enough to quieten even further the already almost stillborn silence . . . and we would continue our mime and our speech in the tranquil Celtic twilight that was the spirit and the secret of the Abbey Theatre.

One afternoon the self-same twilight seemed to have turned itself into a thick mist, stiff with obscurities and the dreams of poets. Down had come the curtain with a smack of despondency on the last

THE MASSINE—LOPOKOVA COMPANY, 1922-3

Left to right: Errol Addison, Lydia Sokolova, Margot Luck, the author,
Massine and Lopokova, Dorothy Coxon, Alice Alonova

THE AUTHOR AS 'CUPID' (1922-3)   *Hana*

RUSSIAN BALLET ROLES

PAPILLON IN 'CARNAVAL

Photo by Vaughan

Bottom left : 'LES BICHES'

Bottom right : 'LES FACHEUX

Photos by Blanc of **Monte Carlo**

rehearsal of *The King of the Great Clock Tower*. The gloom of the theatre was cut off and also those two whispering figures. I arose from my throne and removed my mask, behind which I had sunk for an hour, lulled to peace by the voice of that great actor Peter McCormack. Within the folds of his costume of the heroic age, he looked at me, sighed and shook himself like a dog. 'Well, may the spirit of Mr. Yeats be with us tonight, and may it spread itself a bit and give a clue to the audience as to what it all is that we be talkin' about,' said Peter McCormack, who could not open his mouth but to give a clue to all the mysteries that constitute great acting.

*   *   *

It is a still, late afternoon and Dalkey Bay is in an early summer mind; the Big and Little Sugar Loaf Mountains are in shadow and a splendid blue glow is theirs against the evening sky. I am sitting in the garden of Villa Sorrento, the cliff cottage, and home of the Lennox Robinsons. My companions are Lennox and Yeats. The poet is declaiming certain of his poems. The rich voice rises and falls on the air, an air that is rarefied by the music of the voice in a garden hushed to a gentle static attention. Lennox is motionless, but the glasses once more reflect small shafts of light.

When Yeats died some years later, his old friend spoke of that magic hour and finished his letter to me with the words . . . 'for we have seen Shelley plain.'

They were happy inspiring years; but for me the English scene eventually crowded them out.

Today the greater part of the Abbey awaits reconstruction after the fire of a few years ago. Many of my old friends are dead, or they have retired or emigrated. I last met Barry Fitzgerald and his brother Arthur Shields (who used to be the Abbey stage manager) in Hollywood at a reception given in honour of the Sadler's Wells Ballet in

8

1951. Hollywood had left no mark on these two; the soft brogue remained and the leisured approach to life . . . even in a city dedicated to life in its most hurried form. I lunched with Barry the next day. We were soon back in a Dublin 'of night and light and the half light' as our poet had sung; treading we were on our own dreams of that yesterday.

*   *   *

Fleeting pictures of the late twenties pass before my eyes; at the Old Vic there was the ambitious production of Clemence Dane's play *Adam's Opera* on which Lilian Baylis lost one of those familiar sums of £1,000.

I taught dances to Dame Sybil Thorndike, Dame Edith Evans and to Jean Forbes-Robertson. In *Salome*, I arranged the dance of the Seven Veils first for Vivienne Bennett at Cambridge and later at the Gate Theatre for an actress who could have been just as great a dancer—Margaret Rawlings. I know no actress with a greater sense of natural movement than hers.

I once took the Court Theatre for three matinées of *Ballets for the Repertory Theatre* and lost £200 on the venture. Perhaps it was just as well that in those days I was incapable of taking disaster to heart. A little later I enlisted the aid of the Abbey and the Festival and gave a triple bill with my school. The performance consisted of two plays for dancers and one ballet. This time (as the venture included W. B. Yeats's *Only Jealousy of Emer*) I managed to get out on a loss of about £30 . . . and it was deemed a great success.

During those years I occasionally appeared in London with the Diaghilev Ballet; I also danced with Anton Dolin in a season at the Coliseum coupled with some provincial concerts, and I danced yet again in 1928 in the summer International Opera Season at Covent Garden Opera House. There was, the same year, a disastrous production of a big musical show at His Majesty's Theatre in which I appeared in a ballet, also with Anton Dolin.

In the main I accepted these engagements as a means of making extra money so as to continue my hold on the repertory theatre, for I was convinced that therein lay the future of an English Ballet Company. Such activities, however, meant that I had myself to continue my studies. I looked about for a professor and decided to take three private lessons each week from a certain Madame Zanfretta.

Madame Zanfretta had been a great beauty in her day and a famous Italian mime (it is her traditional method that is now taught at the Sadler's Wells School). She appeared at the Empire for years and now lived in retirement in Hampstead with a married daughter. When she came to my studio she was turned seventy. Erect, handsome, vital and voluble, she was the greatest tonic that I could possibly have found for myself at that time. Her schooling was excellent: soft, flowing and yet extremely strengthening. It was not the rigid Italian system of Cecchetti—it had other influences. She was comfortably off, having always saved. Her husband (who had been a famous animal impersonator) was dead. Madame Zanfretta played only mime rôles after the birth of her daughter; neither she nor the famous animal impersonator considered that the shortened skirt and the low-cut bodice of a dancer's costume were seemly for a wife and mother. But, she brightly informed me, circumstances had permitted her to dance at Covent Garden up to two months before the birth of her daughter, for the condition, she assured me, helped her to balance the pirouettes nicely.

Her feet were severely turned out; the extent and control were such that she could tap with her foot at an angle of forty-five degrees. Everything was either good or bad for the muscles, and no ballerina had any business to sit down in her bath, for it was weakening for muscles. She said neuritis was nonsense; it could only happen because dancers no longer dried their tights in front of big fires, but put them into new-fangled airing cupboards and such things, all bad for the muscles. She had no neuritis, but she had always had a coal fire in her dressing-room, and her tights drying on the guard in front of it. Her muscles were good, they had always been good, and they would remain good.

She began her career when very young in Vienna. She said that she had practised a lot, danced very little, had lived a gay life there and was considered a great beauty. The latter was obvious and the former could certainly be taken for granted. She had wonderful style. I have never seen a more beautiful carriage of head, arms and hands. Her mime was perfection itself; she taught my head teacher, Ursula Moreton, about two hundred gestures, with every detail of footwork and transfer of weight. Her views on modern mime, when expressed, seemed in danger of giving her a stroke. The muscle condition was not exaggerated; once a week this old lady, after my morning lesson, would walk half the way from Gloucester Road to her favourite Italian restaurant in Soho and have her favourite lunch and bottle of chianti before going back to Hampstead.

I introduced her to Lopokova, who was by then married and living in Gordon Square. They got on wonderfully, and 'Zannie', as Lydia would call her, also visited Gordon Square to give the ballerina lessons. She once informed me severely, that she preferred teaching 'Madame Keynes' to me . . . she did not seem so preoccupied, and she had better muscles; she was also very gay and enjoyed getting tired out. But she did add that Madame Keynes never started off as tired as I did; of course, it was obvious that my tiredness was due to 'The Trouble'—her name for the school. She said with my legs and feet I did not need to have a 'Trouble', I should just dance.

She did not approve of the photographs of various productions hanging up in the studio . . . she would stare at one for a long time and then say 'Bogie-Bogie'. However, there was good reasoning behind her muscle bogie. She kept me in better condition than I had been in for years, and I found myself stronger and much better placed under her tuition.

•   •   •

The years have moved on; it is a day in 1930 and I am to visit the theatre on the other side of the river, which is nearly completed.

I go with Miss Baylis in her car. A grey day, with Islington not at its best. We come up the little street near the old river walk. Suddenly, there is consternation in this narrow back street, for out of a door there springs what appears to be Islington's largest rat; he is chased across the street, and with one bound enters the house opposite. This incident, as my introduction to Sadler's Wells Theatre, has never escaped me, for I have a pathological antipathy for rats.

The rebuilding of the old theatre is nearly finished. We go up into the vast circle, which, at this stage, resembles a Roman theatre; there are as yet no seats, only the basic architecture of the circle in skeleton form. It is really very handsome to look at. We enter the ballet room and my spirits rise at the sight of the huge windows and the large, high, airy room. I glance at the floor. 'Is it concrete?' I ask Miss Baylis. She says yes it is concrete, and concrete it will have to be as she has no money for a wooden floor. I do not say anything; but two months later I have the promise of a wooden floor from a private source. Few people know that the wooden floor at the 'Wells Room' was given to the theatre by the late Lady Moyne, whose daughter Grania was one of our students at that time.

I realized at last that all was going to happen according to a dream nearly five years old. The theatre was to be opened by the drama company in January 1931. Miss Baylis wanted the nucleus of the ballet company to be formed by the six girls engaged for the opera ballet, and she wanted the ballet school in the theatre. But there was no money; everything, reasonably enough, had already been allocated to the existing opera and drama company.

I offered her the goodwill of my school, with the condition that, out of the takings, the *corps de ballet* and also my head teacher should be paid. I would keep on Heathfield and work for her free as director, principal dancer and choreographer until the following September.

I then had to produce some accounts showing the school turnover and seek an interview with Sir Reginald Rowe, the Acting Governor of the Old Vic. This charming man, who did so much for us all, saw that I showed a turnover of about £1,200 per annum. This would easily finance the dancers for the next six months, and with free premises, the school housed in the theatre, all would rapidly grow and be in a stronger financial position by the autumn.

I then had to inform the parents, who accepted the scheme with enthusiasm. I sold the remainder of the lease of my studio to another teacher and actually got quite a generous premium for the fittings. With this premium I took a tiny flat in Bloomsbury. I was virtually self-sold to the one institution for which, during nearly five years, I had worked with this one end in view.

It was like coming to the end of a very long tunnel with the sure knowledge that the new countryside was not entirely unfamiliar. The greenest hill, which had taken so long to reach, was now near enough to touch, and in my blissful state of optimism the idea of climbing it seemed to require patience rather than effort.

•   •   •

I must record here that an important part in the early struggling years of both the then Vic-Wells Ballet and the Mercury Ballet Club was played by the Camargo Society, which was, in fact, our Stage Society, and suggested, in the first place, by Philip Richardson and Arnold Haskell.

We were a large, slightly woolly-minded committee, consisting mainly of the dancing profession, with highlights, though, in the form of Maynard Keynes in the chair, Constant Lambert as conductor, Edwin Evans as musical adviser and Montagu Nathan as secretary. On all occasions, Lydia Keynes (still Lopokova to us all) was our most outspoken member. She did not like committees; but having found herself a member of one, she did not suffer from any sense of inertia or inhibition. Her outbursts of thinking aloud very often succeeded in removing hours of wasteful discussion—dedicated in the main to getting us nowhere. When she considered that I had been too reserved over some point of policy she would say severely, 'you are a diplomat . . .' but the tone would not have flattered any aspiring diplomatic figure.

Some famous ballets saw the light of day through the energies of the Society, backed by the sanguine hopes of Keynes, and the enthusiasm of all dancers, choreographers and students. *Façade*, *Pomona* and *Job* were three of these early successes. The smaller works were mounted mainly on the Ballet Club, the larger ones on the Vic-Wells; the two groups inevitably borrowed from each other's reserves, and sought the help of other dancers as well. Money, of course, was desperately short; we performed only on a Sunday night and the following Monday afternoon, restricting our activities to about three programmes every year.

A Camargo production always had its one theatre rehearsal on the Friday preceding the Sunday night performance. *Job*, needless to say, proved to be a particularly difficult proposition as the lighting and staging had to be done at the same time as the orchestral rehearsal. We had been through the ballet once, and there was just enough of our particular orchestral time left to do about one-third of it again. As far as I was concerned it did not matter which part we did repeat; it was all so bad and needed so much more work. Lambert, it appeared, was applying the same unhappy attitude to the score. We started again from the opening scene and got as far as we could before our time was up.

I can remember clutching the rails of the orchestra pit; I did not dare to turn round and face my fellow companions of the Camargo Committee, for I was so deadly ashamed of the scene of chaos that I had just witnessed. I was convinced that the lack of rehearsal was only one fault—I had undoubtedly failed miserably with the work choreographically.

On Saturday morning my drooping spirits received much comfort from two sources; the first was a touching and generous gesture on the part of one British composer to another. Gustav Holst had been present at the rehearsal and I was told that he had been so distressed at the lack of rehearsal for his colleague's great work that he had arranged, under the stipulation of secrecy, to pay for a three hours' orchestral rehearsal on the Sunday morning, at which the Company was also to be present. Secondly, William Chappell told me that Ashley Dukes had been present at the chaotic Friday rehearsal, and that later he had spoken enthusiastically of the whole nightmare. By Monday afternoon Sir Nigel Playfair had written to tell me how much he had liked it.

The hardship and difficulty of getting *Job* produced (in spite of his magnificent performance, Dolin could only give me three rehearsals —I mounted the rôle of Satan on a young boy in the *corps de ballet*) had knocked all courage and objectivity of outlook out of me. I regarded the event with dread and I pictured it as my choreographic 'swan-song'. The English dancers concerned were wonderful: most of the extras came from the Ballet Club and various ballet schools, or they were professional dancers working elsewhere; one and all, they had unselfishly given me what time they could spare over the weeks of spasmodic rehearsal. One of the most conscientious of my 'angels' was Wendy Toye.

The Camargo's biggest effort was a short season of one month at the Savoy, when it presented many of the productions that it had mounted.

It was an odd stroke of fortune that resulted in the Camargo Society first helping the Vic-Wells and finally the Vic-Wells helping the Camargo.

By 1933 the ballet at Sadler's Wells was fairly firmly settled in its policy at the Islington theatre and had an audience that was growing in numbers weekly. The finances of the Camargo had reached a very low ebb: it was felt that the work they had set out to do was accomplished, and justified but now redundant. Maynard Keynes decided that somehow its existing debts must be cleared: this would then allow the venture to shut down and distribute its ballets between the Vic-Wells and the Mercury Ballet Club. He organized two performances at the Royal Opera House, Covent Garden; they were to be given for the delegates of the Economic Conference which was meeting in London that year. The programme chosen was *Lac des*

Cygnes (Act II) and *Coppélia*, as by then both these ballets were in the repertoire of the Vic-Wells. In *Lac des Cygnes* the Swan Princess was danced by Markova and in *Coppélia* there was Lopokova as Swanhilda—she had already danced the rôle for us as a guest artist at Sadler's Wells.

A large sum of money was raised and the Camargo Society closed down after its five years of work—with all debts fully discharged. We were the richer by several important ballets. Our two Covent Garden performances were hardly on a scale that was worthy of the great theatre that we graced for the first time—but it was rather astonishing that we could venture to enter its portals at all after two years of life. We were hailed by Richard Capell in the *Daily Telegraph*—both kindly and poetically—as 'The Islington Dancers'.

•　　•　　•

For the next four years after the opening of Sadler's Wells, I lived in Bloomsbury, making my way daily through its streets and squares towards Sadler's Wells. Around me there gradually formed a Bloomsbury contingent of the ballet. Within two years, Frederick Ashton was a near neighbour, Michael Somes eventually reached Lloyd Square, and Ursula Moreton lived in Mecklenburgh Square. A lovely neighbourhood that was never depressing: we became North Londoners, with our lives and our interests centred on a theatre that boasted, at that time, of a sixpenny gallery.

I have no reason, thank goodness, to dwell in strict detail on the history of those years, for they have been well and truly recorded several times already. Again I shall half close my mind's eye and allow the telling moments that are indelibly imprinted there to speak for me. Personalities perhaps come first.

There was Markova; this tiny, prim little girl whom I had befriended in Russian Ballet days was now with me. She was a true ballerina in all but her repertoire. 'The Wells' had the good fortune to launch her in *Giselle*, in a full *Casse-Noisette* and in *Lac des Cygnes*. These ballets have shown forth her greatness ever since.

I think of all the artists that I have ever encountered she is the most self-reliant. Her strength of purpose and her courage run deep: when Alice says very quietly that something does not matter, that it is quite all right, she means, in one sense, exactly the opposite—for she does not trouble to explain that she considers it her own concern to set about rectifying the matter in question; what is significant is that Alice has, on such occasions, already won, yet all that she appears to do is to retreat like a well-conducted mole. When the opposition has become breathless (and seemingly proved to be in the right) there appears, in the foreground of an apparently smoothed-out landscape, a formidable mound—right in the pathway of any further direct progress: Alice has travelled along her personally constructed underground passage, biding her time and choosing her moment to erect her mound, which is smoothly rounded and of the right size; it is large enough gently to distract and firm enough to demand everyone's respectful attention.

In the past she had constituted by far the most formidable opposition that any vigorous and vocal Russian ballerina has ever had to challenge. She never surrendered; she did not surmount so much as surf-ride—timing the breakers and riding them with breath-taking ease, having, of course, first told everyone that the breakers did not matter and that she had not noticed them. Her dancing portrays the gentle but firm, precise yet fluid, lines of her character: effortless on the surface, yet submitted fundamentally to an iron control; she has a mind that is logical, and an outlook that is steadfast in its sincerity, integrity and loyalty to her art and her friends. She makes no enemies; in her difficult moments she can temporarily exasperate, or inspire good-humoured ridicule; on all occasions, however, she commands everyone's affection, admiration and feeling of good comradeship.

There was the morning when I went up into the Wells Room to see the junior girls, including some new arrivals. My eye swept round and settled on one. Lovely child, I mused, with her elegant limbs and well-poised head. There is something about her though; she does not look English with those almond-shaped eyes. I inquired in a whisper about the little girl who looked Chinese. I asked where she came from and I was told Shanghai. I flashed a look of triumph at Miss Moreton and returned to my inspection. Chinese or not it was obvious that something wonderful and beautiful had come into our midst: not even the proof of a Yorkshire-born father and a mother of Irish descent could shake off this mysterious glamour. 'Little Hookham', who answered to the name of Peggy, grew up into Margot Fonteyn, with her beauty and her mystery surrounding her like a cocoon out of which she never forced a way towards some more spectacular birth. She wore her mystery as a simple birthright, yet as an Empress would bear herself under a load of Crown Jewels that had come her way by right of heritage. In those days, her danc-ing had a colt-like quality, the smile was embarrassingly wide and guileless, the eyes danced. Elegance, however, was discernible, even beneath the careless breadth of adolescent movement. Children are generally either gauche or graceful; Miss Hookham was both—in spite perhaps of a remarkable inner poise: a poise that could only, at this particular period, prove itself through the fact that the gauchery and gracefulness never fell out of step.

She was nervous and sensitive, yet spirited; she would laugh when she was really much nearer tears, and become hopelessly stubborn through sheer fright. Her intelligence and the unfolding of her refined sensitivity welled up from a deep source within her; at one period it actually arrested the projection of herself as an artist, so strong was the impact of certain truths on her mental and emotional development. Such moments of hesitation necessitated a pause in time, and on my part an earnest conversation with Mother and a waiting for the mood to pass. She never failed to come out of such moments stronger and more refreshed, even if those surrounding her felt just a little bit limp. She did not really care if she came to the Wells or not; yet she stayed to care for it with the greatest loyalty that an artist has ever shown.

I am in the same room again on another day. I have received a letter from Margaret Rawlings telling me of a young man she has seen in Australia; she tells me she is sure that he has something very special in him and that he is coming to see me. I look up and see a figure standing in the doorway. Portrait of a young man, very pale, with large eyes; he is wearing a huge camel-hair coat. I am struck by a resemblance in some strange way to Massine. He comes forward and speaks to me very politely—it appears that he has been waiting downstairs for some time. Instinctively I know that this is Margaret Rawlings's Australian find. Everything about him proclaims the artist born. I get on the 'phone to Miss Baylis a little later and beg to be allowed to engage him at once.

Robert Helpmann has always been to me the perfect example of an artist who knows the meaning of theatre. He can time a movement, an expression, or a gesture to perfection. With him, humour is instinctive; he can be the perfect master of understatement. For me, in everything that he has danced there have been great highlights, sometimes only tiny, telling gestures, but these will always remain a part of my greatest theatrical memories.

Nature's artists in the theatre are few and far between, and Helpmann is one of them. He must have been a monstrous child, but endowed with an imagination that put all my 'thinks' to shame. There was the 'family' that lived under a gutter grating, with whom he would have long conversations on his way back from school. They were a large 'family' and they lived just under the grating. The small schoolboy would squat on the kerb beside their home and talk to them, and this made him consistently late in getting back to his own home. There was the highly dramatic note left for the parents saying that he was running away, but the flight was arrested to buy some crystallized pineapple which was eaten on a park bench; this sticky substance somewhat mellowed life, so after a lapse of time reckoned to be long enough to frighten everyone, he returned home. There was the day when he cut school altogether, only to run into Mother round an unfrequented corner. The born actor and agile monkey wit did not falter: Helpmann, with round, staring, protruding eyes, gazed blindly beyond Mother; he was hustled home gently but firmly, suffering from loss of memory.

We will not deny that the monkey tricks and the imagination continued through later life. We suffered gladly, though, the invention of a rather grand touring *prima donna*, who had a landlady named Mrs. Snodgrass (the latter was a true life name, an inspiration discovered on tour); these inventions enlivened many a train journey, for we would be given the highlights of a day in Mrs. Snodgrass's select theatrical digs. There was also the terrible North Country mother 'spoilt by the war' with her son Willie (obligingly played by Constant Lambert) who droned, groaned and grumbled her way across England on those slow wartime trains. These characters grew more and more alive in their sordid topicality and we would await their further eccentricities with the greatest impatience.

I am guilty of encouraging Helpmann's interpretation of Dr. Coppelius up to the height of its utmost humour. Great clowns are rare and Helpmann clowned Dr. Coppelius with genius—sharply outlining the old man's stupefying senility with nonsensical detail. He laid bare those flashes of guile shown by wicked, frustrated old men, who call on their wiles to offset their loneliness, in a world they have set against them.

There was Harold Turner, one of our very finest virtuosity dancers. Before coming to London he started to dance in his native Manchester. I like the story of him, as a boy of fourteen, in his first job in a printing house, cycling swiftly across Manchester directly after working hours, so as to be on time for his dancing lesson at a local school. He was not the star turn at this school; that enviable position appeared, to those in authority, to be more within the possibilities of his sister. During a tour of the provincial towns, Anton Dolin saw Harold Turner and his sister dance in Manchester; he did not encourage the idea that the girl had outstanding talent, but he did advise the parents to send the boy at once to London for serious training.

Michael Somes hailed from the West Country. When I received a letter about him, I was astonished to note that it was written by a headmaster: a discerning headmaster, for this boy was the first to warrant the bestowal of a special scholarship at Sadler's Wells. This particular scholarship had been offered to us by a member of the audience to encourage boy students. It was allotted to Somes, whose talents were matched by his earnest manner and his great ambition.

Pamela May at the age of fourteen was a beautifully made, graceful and talented handful. Her teacher ruefully wrote to the effect that, to discipline her, she must go to the Wells! Pamela settled down—first to a long and distinguished career in the company, and then to pass her knowledge on to the younger Wells generation.

There was June Brae—serious and exotic, who had studied with the same teacher as Fonteyn in China; Elizabeth Miller, Mary Honer, Hermione Darnborough were all among the younger set at the Wells in those early days. There was also one tiny girl in the children's afternoon class. Sheila McCarthy (who taught the youngest scholars) told me that she did not know what to make of this child. I asked her what was the trouble, and the trouble appeared to be that this child could 'do' everything. I visited the class to see this nine-year-old prodigy. I found a tiny scrap of a child with very long limbs, a round cheerful baby face and a mop of short brown curls. She certainly 'did' everything, including a faultless entrechat six. We moved her up two classes, and, to avoid overstrain, halved all her work; she cheerfully continued to hold her own, with a nonchalant ease and an engaging smile. Little Miss Groom eventually grew into Miss Grey, who on her fifteenth birthday 'did' the whole of *Lac des Cygnes* and spent most nights, at that time, in an Anderson shelter in bomb-peppered Croydon.

When Markova joined us in 1932, a decision to mount the classics in honour of an English ballerina ripe to dance them led to a ten years' contract between the Wells and Nicolai Sergueeff. This gentleman was the late *régisseur* of the Marinsky Ballet, Petrograd; he had already produced *Giselle* for the Camargo Society. I learnt from Lydia Lopokova that he was living—or rather starving—in Paris. After she had conducted the preliminary negotiations on our behalf with a series of letters in Russian, I went over to Paris with Miss Baylis's secretary, Evelyn Williams, to engage Sergueeff to produce *Coppélia*, *Lac des Cygnes*, *Giselle* and *Casse-Noisette* for the Sadler's Wells Ballet. We found him in an obscure studio that he shared with another Russian teacher. The necessary contract was drawn up, and a few weeks later he arrived with his tin trunks full of his notation-books; trunks which he had, in some mysterious way, managed to bring out of Russia with him.

Sergueeff was a strange little man. He had experience and tradition, yet he could also show ignorance and prejudice. He taught well enough in an orthodox way, and his notation was a complete and comprehensive system to anyone who had studied it as he had. He meticulously reproduced the choreography on our small company, complaining from time to time of our small numbers and the stage's lack of mechanical devices. He found my indifference to his mechanical requests rather strange, for he could not grasp that it was the choreography that was my principal concern at that moment, and not dozens of cardboard mechanical swans. I would be pre-occupied with recording the human swan evolution and patterns, only to find Sergueeff more concerned with a contraption made of lines of string that would guide the cardboard swans safely across the lake. Nothing would deter him from this pastime that gave him the appearance of being absorbed in some ancient form of cat's-cradle. Time and again, with growing persistence, his cardboard swans would disappear, head first, their tails still visible; the picture resembled ducks ducking for a juicy morsel of underwater life. He gave in though when the chief swan, crowned with her special regal head-dress, decided to turn turtle in midstream. . . .

Beyond manipulating bits of string; winding cardboard wheels; demanding little trucks with wheels disguised as shells; insisting on innumerable swords, red beards for all villains, endless snow; placing rostrums where there was no room for a footstool; wailing for pages and trains edged with ermine—Sergueeff was completely devoid of any real stage sense. The production side, concerning entrances and exits, or the evolutions of human beings in the form of crowd work, had always to be dealt with by me on the quiet. He was unmusical to a degree bordering on eccentricity; he always carried a blue pencil, and would carefully pencil out a bar of music, which, for some reason, wearied him. The offending bar would receive a long, strong blue cross through it. This would mean that I must 'phone Constant Lambert, who would come down in the lunch break and put the bars back. Sergueeff would return, and because, in his absence, I had extended some small choreographic movement to cover Mr. Lambert's tracks, he would be unaware that the position was musically where it had been before the onslaught of the blue pencil! Crotchets would become quavers by the simple process of humming emphatically what he considered a reading of the piano score; this would lead to a show-down with Constant Lambert, and result in Sergueeff sadly murmuring, 'Mr. Lambert . . . he no good.'

Nicolai Sergueeff, however, was a charming old gentleman; his Mongolian features, his store of reminiscences, his shrewd observations on our dancers, and his able casting of them for various rôles, made him a picturesque and much liked personality in our lives. When he got too involved over his mechanical inventions, and his demands for supers exceeded standing room on the Wells stage, I would refer him to Lydia Lopokova: in a vigorous flow of Russian his former pupil would make him see sense, and lighten the burden of my responsibilities. She was fond of him, and would tell me that at the Marinsky Theatre he had been much feared. He would not take bribes, she would add solemnly; it seemed that ladies of the ballet would sometimes try to get protectors to square ballet masters for coveted little solo tit-bits.

·   ·   ·

The years passed swiftly: by 1935 we had a strong company of young dancers and a big school. Money though was very short and salaries low. It was becoming extremely important that the Company find some work out of season, in those months that stretched from May to September. We needed to tour, but tours needed a financial

TWO STUDIES FROM 'LES NOCES' MONTE CARLO (1923)

LILIAN BAYLIS, C.H., RETURNING FROM A PICNIC

guarantee, and the theatre could not risk the possible loss that might be involved.

I had had experience of one such tour with Markova and Dolin just before the former left me in the summer of 1935, and I knew how it had benefited the Company. We now had a greatly enlarged Company, with Frederick Ashton as resident choreographer, Pearl Argyle, the young Fonteyn, Helpmann, Turner, Somes, May, Brae, Honer, Miller, Chappell, Gore and Newman; there was a fair-sized *corps de ballet*, all graduates from the Wells School.

One day I was asked by Miss Baylis to speak about the ballet at a large gathering of people in a house in Belgrave Square. Tyrone Guthrie was to speak on the drama, and Sir Reginald Rowe on the opera and the theatre in general. I outlined my own policy and stressed the importance of more employment for the dancers out of season. I particularly emphasised that these young artists needed a bigger guarantee of security if we were to hold them together throughout the year.

A few days later I received a letter from the secretary of a lady who had been present at the Belgrave Square meeting. The letter said that the lady had been very much impressed by my appeal, and that my approach to the problems of the ballet met with her sympathy and understanding. She found my attitude constructive and she wanted to meet me. Would I have lunch with her? That lunch was, for me, to prove as lucky as my first crossing of the Waterloo Bridge: this lady, who was exceedingly wealthy, offered at the end of our first meeting to guarantee the necessary financial support for the ballet and orchestra for their next summer tour. Her solicitor met Miss Baylis and the theatre's solicitors a few days later. She backed the ballet on all its provincial tours for two years, after which we were sufficiently established to take care of ourselves and we did not have to call again on her generosity.

My benefactress has been dead for many years. She expressed a wish to remain anonymous, and I feel that I must still respect her request. But she played an important part in helping the Sadler's Wells Ballet during a very difficult time, and was also the means,

9

through the ballet, of giving regular summer employment to the Sadler's Wells orchestra. I remember expressing to her my personal distress at the sum of money lost on the first tour; she asked me the exact amount of money earned in salaries by both ballet and orchestra during the seven weeks' work. It was at least eight times the amount lost. She then pointed out that such earnings, coupled with the cultural importance of the tour, turned her loss into moneys that she considered well invested. To my delight, on our second tour, we had only to call on her for the modest sum of £200.

•   •   •

I can still see in retrospect the pattern of our lives in those Bloomsbury years. Until I married in 1935 I lived within a few hundred yards of Gordon Square, and was a member of the Bloomsbury ballet contingent. 46 Gordon Square, the home of the Keynes family, was for me and for other dancers a refuge from everyday life. Lydia and Maynard took on themselves, as it were, the care of the British Ballet. The Camargo Committees also met at this house and I went there for advice in all my troubles. Young impecunious artists were given many splendid luncheons and suppers there with wine to wash the meal down. Lydia now informed me that what mattered on the domestic front was the possession of fine linen. Hats by then undoubtedly took a back seat in her life. Her large dining-room table was always covered with superb snowy-white damask cloths, accompanied by those generous-sized white napkins of a bygone day; fine bed-linen and towels I would also be requested to inspect. If Maynard were away, red wine would still be left out for us to drink, with instructions as to warming it. Lydia would always carry out his instructions with great gravity, but sometimes the heat of the argument would be uppermost in her mind; a great shout would herald the return of her thoughts to the business of hospitality and our glasses would be filled to the brim with gently steaming wine! We would await its cooling, our Philistine appetites unaffected, with the possible exception of Constant Lambert, who alone was the real connoisseur of food and drink present.

Constant Lambert, the architect of English Ballet music, was a figure prominent amid all our triumphs and disasters. The domestic picture conjured up by memory shows him in the ever shabby overcoat, complete with his stick, a score under one arm, a tattered newspaper peeping from his pocket, and the inevitable cigarette spraying his waistcoat with a cloud of fallen ash. Yet resolute and stalwart is the same figure on the rostrum, attired for many evenings of those early years in a morning coat that had once been the property of his father. I have seen him wield his baton on occasions both great and small, with an intensity that no circumstances diminished. He bestowed the same attack and energy on his piano playing during the early period of the war, resolute always that the best only should come forth from the orchestra pit.

Genial as a good-natured schoolboy, he was as much at home in a third class railway carriage playing cards on the back of a music score (or on a crumpled *Times* drawn forth from the pocket of the ancient overcoat) with the humblest members of the Company, as in the presence of his particular cronies in the red plush of the old Café Royal.

He detested humbug, and any form of false pride or intellectual snobbery. Helpmann's mimicry of anyone or anything left him prostrate with merriment; he would spend hours with the Company, playing absurd games and listening to equally absurd stories; he adored finding himself solemnly billed at the Bournemouth Pavilion as Constance Lambert, and again on an ENSA tour, as Miss Constance Lambert at the Piano.

Loved by every orchestra player in London, he became a symbol of security when he entered the orchestra pit. As for the dancers, Constant in charge meant to them that all was well with the world; as director, I would sink back with a sigh of relief at the sight of the alert back and the raised arm—the signal for an onslaught of the surest of sure beats. It was Constant Lambert's baton that started the conquest of New York on a hot and humid evening at the 'Met' in

1949; it keyed the Company to a pitch that I have never seen them surpass.

A vision of Constant again, after more Irish whisky than was good for him: it is moonlight, late at night, on the deserted deck of the Dublin mail boat, and the sea is suddenly bespattered with bobbing, rakish-looking wicker armchairs, rocking and tossing in the middle of the Irish sea. Leaning over the rails, waving them a genial farewell, is the Maestro; he had pitched them overboard, having found them smug and offensive-looking on the deck. Now they appeared relaxed and friendly, dipping and faintly protesting at their loss of dignity. He wished them no harm upon the Irish waters; he no doubt meant them to reach the shores of his much-loved Dublin in preference to Liverpool; for such was his benevolence. He just did not like the look of them on board, nor did he think it possible that the atmosphere of the first class lounge of the mail boat was conducive to wicker-chair development of character.

I knew Constant when he was very young; I was in Paris, on a short engagement with the Russian Ballet, at the time he was having his first ballet produced by no less than the Diaghilev Company. During the Monte Carlo rehearsals there had been a row: Constant had defied Diaghilev in support of the choreographer, Nyjinska. The young man went so far as to threaten that he would take himself off, and with him his score. Later he would tell, with delight, of his astonishment at the sight of his score, heavily guarded by two of the casino gendarmes, in picturesque musical comedy uniforms, on its voyage from music library to rehearsal rooms! Diaghilev was the true autocratic Russian; he was not used to threats and displays of nonchalant independence: this fresh-complexioned young Englishman was treated with grave suspicion—he was either a revolutionary or else queer in the head. Again, Diaghilev could not, as a Russian, imagine the delight that the spectacle of this guard of honour gave Constant, making it impossible for him to carry out a threat that would spoil a good story.

By chance rather than intent, I was in the cast, soon after the opening night of Lambert's *Romeo and Juliet*; being thrust on as the nurse, as Sokolova was ill. I appeared in the scene connected with the Monte Carlo dispute; consequently, it had no music, and had been choreographed by Balanchine—by Diaghilev's orders! On the opening night of the ballet, Paris staged a theatrical *scandale* unequalled for noise. I can remember the Company's feeble attempt to start the ballet; gendarmes charging down the centre aisles hitting out right and left; gendarmes appearing at the rear of the boxes, and seizing protesting members of the *avant-garde* or the '*garde*' no longer '*avant*' (the argument was very complicated) by the back of their necks, and dragging them forth into the cool night air. In five minutes all was peace; the ballet returned to the beginning, and the curtain rose with dignity and a studied air of forgetfulness as to its earlier less dignified descent: thus Constant Lambert's first ballet was born, under the patronage of a smart Parisian first night audience, complete with a well-staged *scandale* dear to the heart of the French theatre, and a stormy passage behind the scenes.

His early death was a tragedy: doubly so because his life had a defiant, reckless quality that tended to interfere with the fine balance of his more considered judgements on all subjects and people. It was not a life that had attained anything like the full development of its genius. A death such as his leaves a deep feeling of frustration; having sensed so much promise, we are poorer than ever in being cheated of the full fruits of such talents; we are left aware of a heritage that is lost, for we have no means of recognizing the heir-apparent and so living on the hopes of a future fulfilment. If the hand of destiny had been less wayward, Lambert would not only have fulfilled himself, but, equally important for this mundane selfish world, he would have led and inspired the younger generation.

He seemed an Englishman of another and more full-blooded day, perhaps because he was an Edwardian in both life and thought. Behind and beyond it all he was an intensely humane and kindly person. He had friends in every walk of life; his life had many by-ways, wherein he sought out these friendships, and one and all revelled in his sagacious and virile company.

The mind was a brilliant one: up to the very end that mind could rear itself above us all. Witness the contents of his last score *Tiresias*, which shows a powerful intellect at work that not even illness could overthrow. I know that many will agree with me when I say that in Lambert lay our only hope of an English Diaghilev.

·   ·   ·

A brief, sharp picture of Gordon Square in the 'thirties almost defies my memory, yet I can just discern it. A winter evening, and I am at No. 46; it is the drawing-room and *tableaux vivants* and theatrical playlets are in progress. The curtain parts: it reveals Lydia and Maynard—but it is also 'Victoria and Her Albert'. By this time, Bloomsbury has discovered Lydia's undoubted resemblance. What an audience! In silhouette I can recognize the following heads: Lytton Strachey, G. B. Shaw, Clive Bell, Duncan Grant, Vanessa Bell, Roger Fry, Virginia Woolf—all Bloomsbury in force—to complete the picture of those years.

Maynard Keynes by 1936 had built the Cambridge Arts, as a successor to the Festival Theatre. At the opening production of the Festival, my school in South Kensington had supplied dancers for the Greek chorus in the *Orestia*. Ten years later, and a young but fair-sized English Ballet Company was to open this new repertory theatre at Cambridge.

·   ·   ·

I dwell again on those Islington days . . . there was the Gertrude Stein-Frederick Ashton-Lord Berners *Wedding Bouquet* production, complete with the Vic-Wells chorus. Lilian Baylis and Gertrude Stein taking a call together—a delicious sight that was much to the liking of the audience. There was a great bond of sympathy between these two. 'The Lady' found 'the Stein' most intriguing.

Other small adventurous productions livened up our lives that were, more generally, heavily encumbered with the production of the full-length classics for a handful of silver and with a pocketful of dancers: there was also Sergueeff to cope with, who considered (not unjustly) that he was busy coping with us. Once we had headlines in an evening paper—'Bloomsbury Ballet for the Highbrows for 9d.' —an allusion to the current production—the Duncan Grant décor and costumes for Doone's *Tombeau de Couperin*, and our modest gallery entrance price. My own production of *Création du Monde* (Milhaud) with décor and costumes by Edward Wolfe (inherited from the Camargo) appealed to the minority and enraged the majority; Miss Baylis, I fear, heavily on the side of the majority.

I remember a visit to our ballet on the part of the great Toscanini: *Checkmate* made a deep impression on the Maestro. I met him next morning in the theatre's office: he took my hand between both of his, but beyond one word—'Bravo'—I did not understand what he said to me. The fine face, though, was alight with sincere pleasure. I was told later that he had alluded to it as his favourite ballet.

Slowly, our more severe critics decided that, with the assistance of the classics, the Bloomsbury set and our growing English repertoire of ballets, we were bearable between September and May—when there were no Russians to view at Covent Garden.

It was the death of Diaghilev and Pavlova that gave English Ballet an odd sense of release and the sudden loss of a hopeless feeling of inferiority; yet it was the revival of Russian Ballet, as the Ballet de Monte Carlo, that, while making life for the Vic-Wells in 1933 stiff with uphill work and crushing any possible feeling of complacency, bestowed on us one great asset: there was now the new popular public that the young Russians were creating in the West End of London, as well as the smaller public which we had also built up on the heights of Islington and on the South Bank; all three contingents showed signs of joining forces 'out of season'—in other words our season at Sadler's Wells from May to September. We noted that the Russian Ballet gallery and amphitheatre regulars were making pilgrimages to the Wells; they either stayed to swell our regular audience, or went their way elsewhere shaking their heads; in the latter case, it was over that sad, bad thing—the hopeless case of the English Ballet. . . .

The very early Islington years had their guest artist list of already established famous names—Lopokova, Bedells, French, Dolin and Idzikowsky; Markova became the first resident ballerina, and lovely Pearl Argyle was a regular member of the Company for two years from 1935 to 1937. The same year (1935) Ashton joined us as our first full-time choreographer.

The legion of Sadler's Wells dancers, who today are household names, springs from our own modest enough sowing of 1931—but somehow it had sufficient depth to be able to withstand the violent efforts at uprooting of the 'forties.

Covent Garden Opera House continued, even in the 'thirties, to re-enter my life from time to time. There is one more auspicious occasion to remember—the State Visit of the French President (Monsieur Lebrun) in the spring of 1939. On this occasion, the 'Islington Dancers', in conjunction with Sir Thomas Beecham and the Philharmonic Orchestra, put on two acts of *The Sleeping Beauty*; this ballet had just been mounted at Sadler's Wells with décor and costumes by Nadia Benois. Again it must be noted that we were not really ready; it was impossible to transpose with complete success our modest Sadler's Wells effort (which looked so opulent in its own theatre!) to the vast dimensions of Covent Garden. It left us critically aware of the long way ahead, and inevitably brought a certain amount of adverse criticism on our heads. Nevertheless, at the same time, it considerably enhanced our position; for it showed the charitably-minded members of the audience that they must now reckon with rather more than translation of an English ballet.

•   •   •

The life of the young Sadler's Wells Ballet developed a remarkably even rhythm during the 'thirties. Provincial tours in the latter part of the summer: Sadler's Wells from September to May; then

Bournemouth, Oxford and Cambridge before the summer holidays.

Vividly I can see a splendid, early summer day in Cambridge, spent on the College backs with a number of the Company. A sudden sense of isolation came to me and a sharp question ruthlessly thrust itself into the foreground of my mind. The question was never expressed openly, but that did not deter its melancholy persistence throughout the day. It was concerned with the events that would occur to break up this present life and scatter all these young people elsewhere. I felt a poignant certainty that their simple state of existence together could not last. . . .

．　　　．　　　．

I am on tour again. I see a great stretch of time covering a space of twenty-five years and one month: yet the pattern of my life decrees that I shall be on tour once more—on the eve of the second world war.

．　　　．　　　．

It is Liverpool: a city given up to mad anticipation, and encased every night in a clumsy, noisy dress rehearsal of a blackout. The skies, night and day, are persistently overcast, and are deeply occupied with awkward, as yet amateurish efforts to send up full-bellied, grey, elephant-like balloons. The skies appear to hold their breath, in an effort to uphold these monsters; on their wires the elephants sway self-consciously and rebelliously; they look despondent and without confidence in their mission. The public eyes them with derision and little sense of comfort or security. Silently, night after night, the Company go about their performances in the morose half-filled theatre. In my hotel are the great Karsavina and her husband, back from Hungary and filled with a profound sense of the inevitability of what is coming, for they know something of the state of Europe.

It is early Sunday morning, 3rd September. Mechanically and half-heartedly we have boarded our train for Leeds. I stand in the corridor with Ashton. The station is crowded with bewildered women and children about to be evacuated and now under the care of efficient welfare officers. The women and the children all have a destination; the women's is written on paper in their handbags and in their sad, puzzled faces, the children's on bright optimistic-looking labels tied to their clothes. One young woman can be seen to sink on to her luggage holding close to her a small baby; she starts to shake out her handkerchief. 'Don't cry, you poor thing,' murmurs Ashton, thinking aloud . . . but she had decided that that was all that was left for her to do.

We are half-way on our journey across this changed England; we reach a small station and see a special poster: it reads, 'War Declared'.

One night is spent in Leeds. It is as though we had arrived in a dead town—the theatres read 'Closed by Order of the Home Office'. We creep to our hotels and lodgings. Most of the night is spent in a cellar with our gas masks most self-consciously packed in their little boxes: a lone plane has been sighted over the North Sea and the sirens burst forth in righteous triumph, piercing the empty, dark, silent streets and sending us all, like obedient rats, down to the cellars.

We reach London next afternoon and disperse until further notice. Bar one, it is the most gloomy homecoming that the Company is ever to experience.

V

THE WIND IN THE CLOCK

The wind has at last got into the Clock—
Every minute for itself.
There's no more sixty,
There's no more twelve,
It's as late as it's early . . .
LAURA RIDING

IN WARTIME all actions and thoughts become congested and condensed; we develop a new conception of time—an isolated existence which is born, consumes itself fiercely and dies within the period of years that the war takes to spend itself. Constantly we are assailed by a nostalgia for the immediate past; our arrested mainstream of life becomes our only refuge from our artificially constructed present: a present that forbids us to dwell on any project that is outside the demand of the furious moment. Later, when we can discard this compressed-steam existence, we find ourselves confronted with change: the phenomenon has disrupted the return to our real way of life—that way of life which during the war years suffered the fate of the Sleeping Beauty.

It is a broken picture that I am piecing together: it is laid out on the floor of my mind and resembles the component parts of a disintegrated jig-saw puzzle. I finger one piece which has an outline that holds promise; I search with impatience for another that is likely to go with it; to assemble the pieces is my ambition, and thus reconstitute a picture that I once laid by in the storeroom of my mind. Memory, though, is not helpful; the individual piece may well be the vivid recollection of a single moment in the past, a moment severed so roughly from all that preceded and followed that its replacement in the picture, at a later date, is difficult.

•   •   •

There was something extremely touching and poignant about the Company during the first year of the war: the boys, philosophically awaiting the call-up of their age groups, brought a sense of zealous dedication to the work in general. This mood, however, was often punctuated by stretches of despondency and irritable unrest. The artists were confronted with minimum salaries, drastic reductions of scenery and lights, two pianos replacing the orchestra and endless touring. Sunday travelling became an affair of long waits on sidings, sitting on suitcases in corridors and luggage vans. There was nothing to lighten the load of that sharp, ever present emotional feeling concerning the approaching dismemberment that would rend asunder the life of the Company as a whole.

High up under the roof, in its solitary classroom, the School continued at Sadler's Wells; it was now under my sole tutelage, with the assistance of Sergueeff. The Old Vic and the Sadler's Wells Theatre were left naked and helpless with their heavy overheads and their building debts unsolved; bricks and mortar were the prime cause of the strict economies—for they were to be, from now on, a heavy charge on the opera, ballet and drama companies' earnings up and down the country.

During the autumn tour of 1939 Ashton produced his moving conception of Liszt's *Dante Sonata*. It was the first wartime production, and bore all the signs of that simplicity that was to be the keynote of our work for some time to come. A short winter season at Sadler's Wells in January 1940 brought it to the London public: it was one of our major wartime successes.

•   •   •

It was in the early spring of 1940 that the British Council and the Foreign Office decided to present Holland with a little cultural propaganda in the form of the Sadler's Wells Ballet. The late Lord Lloyd, a great ballet lover, and head of the British Council at that time, was the prime mover in the plan. The venture was considered important enough to justify the call-up due for any male dancers that spring being deferred for two months.

On 4th May we embarked for Rotterdam. We were the only occupants of a small Dutch boat; we travelled tourist and were crowded into as small a space as possible. The dining table was squeezed into a large cabin, with bunks from floor to ceiling; it was here that the male members of the ballet were to sleep. We women had similar sleeping accommodation, but were spared the canteen trimmings. The first-class saloons, cabins and deck promenades were all barricaded off, an arrangement that made it impossible for us to move freely about the boat. It was an unadventurous journey made mainly by night; at boat-drill just before dark we saw the gloomy spectacle of sunken trawlers with their funnels and masts still above water.

Rotterdam greeted us with scintillating sunshine setting off its Dutch cleanliness in the clear morning air. It was, I think, a national holiday: cyclists seemed to be everywhere, with circlets of tulips round their necks and entwined across the handlebars of their bicycles. Life seemed leisurely, and the comforts of life exceedingly plentiful. Our Dutch agents, the Beeks, packed us into a motor bus for the thirty-minute drive to The Hague, where we were to live during the entire ten days' tour of Holland.

It was not unlike coming out of a long, deep sleep: for a brief space of time we had emerged from a country responding to the rhythm of war. Our English nights were governed by an intense blackout, made bearable only by the weapon of the torch, which must be shone on the ground, just a little ahead of each footstep taken. The days were given to coping with rations, restrictions and over-crowding; endless bill-posters appeared saying either: 'Have you got your gas-mask with you?' or 'Is your journey really necessary?'

'Lovely Holland,' we thought, with its bright lights that made our eyes blink at such unaccustomed brilliance. 'Beautiful food!' we exclaimed, at the plates of deep pink ham and the smooth thin-cut slices of Dutch cheese: the butter left us dazed and the sugar ecstatic.

It is our opening night at the charming Hague theatre. How friendly is the audience, and how startling the sight of the Opera House foyer! I find myself suddenly confronted with the delicious formality of full evening dress, a convention already discarded in England to the lumber room of our nostalgic past. Full, voluminous evening dresses in rich, heavy silks, encase Dutch dowagers; they crown their smooth decorous hair-styles with suitable tiaras, and long, luxurious, white kid gloves stretch their way opulently up their well-upholstered arms. Shy, plump daughters in virginal tulle accompany these worthy ladies, escorted by prosperous-looking Dutch fathers, resplendent in tails. Standing at the corner of the foyer I suddenly find myself very near tears: I have been long enough in the country to recognize the outward signs of courage everywhere. I know that every thinking Dutch man and woman is aware that life can change overnight for them, and in a way that years of war may not change England. Tonight they pay their tribute, and express their innermost thoughts for England and her welfare: no matter that these feelings are expressed prosaically in tulle, silk, tiaras and immaculate kid gloves.

A little later in the evening the signs of friendship take on a more poetic note: at the close of the performance a heavy shower of tulip petals falls on the dancers from the roof of the theatre: the cascade seems without end; one imagines those orderly fields of tulips outside breaking ranks and casting themselves from the skies in a gesture of friendly self-abandon . . . the scene has become, with time, a curtain-call that is a shining moment in memory, kept bright and alight by the spirit that prompted it.

Each day found us in our bus travelling along interminably long and straight roads, on our way to some other town where we were due to give a performance: we returned to The Hague, by the same means, in the very early hours of the morning. As the week progressed the general situation appeared to worsen, and this was manifested in a tension and a general restlessness, not to mention alarming rumour. From conversations with the Dutch themselves, it was difficult to make out anything; there was either a fatalistic shrug of the shoulders, or an optimistic allusion to the history of the first world war.

I received my first shock the night that we played in Hengelo.

THE AUTHOR
IN 1931

Photo by Sasha

MME ZANFRETTA

SADLER'S WELLS ROLES IN THE THIRTIES
Above: With Frederick Ashton in 'Barabou'
Right: With Robert Helpmann in 'Douanes'

This was a border town situated in a part of the country that, in case of invasion, was not to be defended. The performance was preceded by a dinner given by that indefatigable institution—the English-Netherlands Society—and I had been invited to be their guest of honour. Just before dinner I was informed by the now very anxious Beeks that all railways were closed. I asked the chairman, a Dutchman, if he considered that it would be wiser for us to depart immediately after the performance. (The British Council had arranged for us to stay the night in this town as it was hours by car from The Hague.) He assured me that there was no need to worry, the closing of the railways in towns so near the German border was a very common occurrence. Nevertheless, I decided on a short night's rest and we left very early in the morning for The Hague.

The week progressed; anxiety mounted; the British Government fell; scraps of news were picked up on the radios, but still we continued to carry out our mission. The Dutch still gave us their full attention and showed, at every performance, their enthusiastic appreciation. At the lovely little theatre of the Phillips' factory the entire audience stood to applaud us at the end of the performance . . . and once more the tulip petals rained down on the dancers' heads.

It is Thursday, 9th May; our objective was Arnhem. On our way the bus passed by a great number of people trudging in the opposite direction . . . peasants dragging children and carrying large bundles of belongings. We gave our performance, and once more, with its steady defiance of gathering clouds, the English-Netherlands Society entertained me before the show. The chairman, a charming Dutch Baroness, was accompanied by an enchanting small daughter. This eight-year-old child had a distinction and personality rare in one so young. Her mother spoke of the child's wish to become a dancer. I remember my reaction: that here a star was born—no matter in what guise. In an ankle-length party dress this child presented me with a bouquet of red tulips; but the tulips are over-shadowed by the elfin grace of the donor and the small face lit up by its promise of character, at present shining forth from a pair of sensitive dancing eyes. I can see her as clearly today in that indelible impression of her

youthful yesterday as the world sees her now in the full flowering of
her young womanhood: her name is Audrey Hepburn.

Concerning our Dutch adventure, memory has now become a
torrent of pinpoint flashbacks: even trivial incidents press urgently
for a hearing: their influence is such that it compels me to record
some of these happenings in chronological order.

Earlier in our Arnhem day I had sat with the wardrobe mistress,
and, to help her, had patched most carefully one of the legs of
Frederick Ashton's *Façade* trousers: it was a large, carefully sewn
patch, just over the knee, for it was executed with a due regard for
the importance of its longevity. However, I have never known how
long my patch did last, or what Germanic dancing knee may eventually have worn it out. I never saw the garment again.

Supper after the Arnhem performance: I can recall how hastily
we ate it and that it consisted of large plates of wonderful ham and
generous helpings of salad. I can remember looking out of a window,
straining my eyes across the flat countryside to the not very distant
horizon, which was German territory. We were bidden to hurry and
to board the waiting bus so as to start our long trek back to The
Hague with all possible speed. The drive was ominous: the roads full
of the Dutch populace deciding on a move towards the coast, and
full equally of Dutch soldiers tramping in the opposite direction to
take up posts of more sinister significance.

It was a dark night that seemed preoccupied with heralding in
Holland's dark tomorrow.

By 3 a.m. we were back at The Hague. By 4 a.m. I was awakened
by a sharp fusillade. From my window, in that cold touch of dawn
on Friday, 10th May, I could discern two planes seemingly trying
to get above each other: even then I did not recognize a dogfight in
progress: I returned to bed faintly irritated by what I presumed to be
Dutch early morning manoeuvres. But there was no more sleep, for
the noise increased. I arose, donned a dressing-gown and went out
into the passage. The hotel was slightly astir, and I ran into a member
of the Company. I expressed some annoyance with Dutch pre-
occupation with war, and with one of those masterly examples of

British understatement, Fanny Spicer made the following reply: 'Excuse me, Miss de Valois, but I really think it must be the Germans.' I went down to the hall porter who left me in no doubt as to the nature of the noise. Holland, he said, had been invaded, and, he added rather cynically, 'You are in for a long stay in my country.'

The rest of that day is fragmentary in my memory: for instance, the arrest of the large German blonde in our hotel, and her descent, an imposing Valkyrie, down the main stairs escorted by two small Dutch soldiers. We were all delighted with our uninhibited view from chairs in the hall lounge! For some days we had eyed her with curiosity in the hotel dining-room. She did not even deign to look our way; one felt that she somehow considered our existence on earth to be no more than a matter of momentary irritation. She had reminded me of a rhododendron in full bloom: now, between two stocky grey-clad figures, I witnessed the fall of her over-luscious petals.

Somewhere about 10 a.m. I was able to get out and visit the British Embassy, where I was greeted with an atmosphere of kindliness and patience, not to mention an intense pre-occupation with bonfires. There were bonfires in the grounds and bonfires in all the fireplaces throughout the reception and secretarial rooms. A modest number of serene, grey-haired ladies of the chancellery appeared to accept the invasion as they might an ambassadorial garden party: both cases naturally meant much extra work to do—with the garden party there would be numerous domestic details to attend to, with an invasion there was the constant feeding of the bonfires with documents and correspondence ensuring that only efficiently charred remains would eventually become the property of the enemy. I returned to the hotel to await, with assumed patience and no bonfires to distract me, news of how and when we might hope to get away.

On my return I heard that early in the morning some of the Company, huddled round a wireless set, had made great efforts to get the B.B.C. They eventually succeeded. England, though, was living according to plan: over the radio was to be heard a bright,

female voice coaxing the British housewife to stick to her daily
dozen. 'Up—down—up—down—little bounce—little bounce—
little bounce—up!' she merrily chanted. Only a little time earlier I
had chased the Company off the hotel roof where they had gone to
witness a fine exhibition of the little bounce—the German para-
chutists coming down in the immediate surroundings of the town;
and on the same roof had been found the following leaflet, fluttering
down in its thousands over The Hague from enemy aircraft:

Strong German troop units have surrounded the city. Resistance is of
no use. Germany does not fight your country but Great Britain. In order
to continue this battle the German Army has been forced to penetrate
your country. The German Army protects the life and goods of every
peace-loving citizen. However, the German troops will punish every deed
of violence committed by the population with a death sentence. Every
citizen is obliged to carry on with his work as usual. Thus he will serve
the interests of his own nation.

A curious lightening in the town's atmosphere came about midday. The morning had been grey and stormy; the loneliness of the
deserted streets in sharp contrast to the noise of the dogfights in the
air, shrapnel descending, and military motor-bicycles and lorries
rushing through the town to other destinations. Now the sun was
out and the cafés filled up; the Dutch bicycle traffic was suddenly in
evidence again in its full force. I sat in the hotel's pavement café with
Lambert and Ashton—but we were driven inside by a stray bullet
which, ricocheting unpleasantly from the pavement, passed between
our heads and crashed through the plate glass of the café window
directly behind us. The bullet had come from a German plane that
had just swooped low over the little square.

Friday night found a tired company sleeping anywhere on the
ground floor of the hotel and up the stairs, for the position was
deteriorating rapidly. By Saturday morning German planes were
roaring over the town, dipping low and sending us all continually
to the ground, flat on our faces: the destruction of Rotterdam had
started; we were aware that this town was only thirty minutes by

car from The Hague and about the same number of seconds by plane. Rotterdam had a death roll of 20,000 inhabitants, The Hague merely got the occasional bomb that was meant for its unhappy neighbour. We gauged the devastating, systematic horror of the attack from the unceasing roar of the planes, passing over in their close, sinister formation.

We were by now confined to the hotel; it was no longer safe outside and we had been informed by the Embassy that we must be ready to leave at a moment's notice. Just before the situation had deteriorated so sharply, I had been once more to the Embassy to collect some money for the journey; I saw Lord Chichester, who was one of the secretaries, and he gave me all that he had—£25. We discussed the situation and studied the map on the wall, which showed how far the Germans had penetrated by land at that moment. During the day several false alarms followed as to when and how we were to leave. At one moment we were informed that we would leave in a fishing smack from Scheveningen, a seaside resort very near The Hague. The fishing smack would be under the command of Admiral Dickens, and, as a matter of interest, we were informed that he was a grandson of Charles Dickens. Nothing came of this plan (which held all the ingredients of a first-class musical comedy), for by the time the crazy venture was decided on, the German para-chutists had landed in a series of buoyant little bounces on our precious beach—thus effectively cutting us off from a taste of the Admiral's seamanship. I met him at the end of the war and he confirmed the authenticity of the story, one that, till then, I had never quite believed!

Late on Saturday afternoon our devoted concert agents came to see us and said that we must immediately make ourselves packets of food; we were also told that one tiny hand suitcase was all that we could take with us. Our main luggage and all personal belongings were to be left behind. It was odd how much consternation this caused! I parted with a silk dressing-gown with more misery than my evening dress, for I knew which of the two I would find the more useful in the ensuing years. Ashton was distraught about his brand-new dinner jacket. I decided that this expensive item of the male wardrobe was large enough for me to wear over my light summer coat and skirt—so one solitary dinner jacket saw England again. We cut our own sandwiches in the hotel kitchen, for the Dutch staff had long left the hotel in a last bid to get back to their homes and families.

Late in the afternoon a man arrived at the hotel and announced brusquely that there was a bus at the door and that everyone was to board it immediately—it was our last chance to get away. It was a horrible moment: I had received strict instructions from the Embassy that on no account was I to accept any form of transport other than that arranged through them. I could see the mute appeal on the still stoically disciplined faces of the Company, yet I had to tell him (with outer conviction but no inner courage) that the Company could not go without the sanction of the Embassy. He asked me irritably what I was waiting for as he was from the Embassy; in fact he happened to be the military attaché. I snapped back, equally irritably, that I could not possibly know that as he was in mufti: I added that he could have said so at the beginning, and saved an argument. Tempers were short by now.

The bus awaited us, complete with an armed guard. It was about six o'clock in the afternoon when we set off for an unknown destination. The deserted streets had about them an unearthly silence and we passed many houses with rifles protruding from their windows. We were all very quiet, for we had just taken a sad farewell of our kindly Dutch agents who had shown such selfless devotion towards the problem of our safety. They stood on the pavement with Lord Chichester waving us good-bye: brave people now facing a future that we had undoubtedly made very much more difficult for them: it was known to everyone how hard they had worked to assist the escape of the English artists.

I see a small square, the bus enters it and turns sharply to the right so as to continue its way down a long street leading out of the town. On the pavement in the middle of the square, and facing this street, I notice that a slab of paving stone has been removed, and a hole dug in the earth beneath. In this hole squats a Dutch soldier, with his rifle pointed down the street—a sniper keeping his lonely vigil. Opposite, on one of the corner houses, hangs a German plane . . . it hangs nose down over the crushed façade of the house—its great wings hopelessly disabled and its body burnt out. Its helplessness has the spent strength of a huge dead eagle: in contrast the motionless little soldier awaiting the coming of his country's enemies appears stolidly alive; he is silent expectancy—in a town suddenly hushed to a silence born of an unbearable suspense.

On and on goes the bus; we leave The Hague far behind us and make for the flat open country. It gets dark: our sandwiches are eaten and we are reduced to watching a long stretch of road and listening to our own thoughts. Great fires light the distant horizon on all sides; the bus continues its monotonous hesitant journey across the immeasurable flatness of the landscape.

Suddenly we are in a wood: the bus comes to a halt among thick trees and we are told to disembark, and stick together. Just before we left The Hague, I decided that, in the event of getting mixed up with other refugees, the Company should be divided into seven groups, each group in charge of a leader who, on all occasions concerned with embarking and disembarking, would announce when his party was complete. Constant Lambert, Frederick Ashton, John Sullivan (our stage director), Claude Newman, Joy Newton, Robert Helpmann and I were the leaders. Leaving the bus in these woods of Velsen on this dark night we hold our second roll-call and thus keep together as we follow a soldier towards a dark, heavily shuttered house. Inside is chaos: the house is crammed with refugees asleep on all available chairs, beds and sofas. On the floor of various rooms our tired groups fling themselves down to fall into weary sleep until morning.

The next morning was bright and sunny; we were given some breakfast and left to our own devices. No one could give us any news or any instructions—it was still a game of waiting. We crowded round a wireless set and got the B.B.C. In England they were interviewing refugees who had just arrived from Holland on the first boats to get away. Highly coloured pictures were painted of the invasion by those who had reached England. The Company was upset: they thought of their friends and relatives and the worry that the exaggerated stories would cause them. I hinted that when they got back they should remember this incident for the sake of others who might still be left behind.

It was strange what that lovely spring day did to change the atmosphere of the previous night. By early afternoon this country house, with its proud peacocks, its artificial lake complete with swans, seemed far removed, in its wooded seclusion, from the turmoil of the rest of the country; our boys even played an impromptu football match in the grounds against the Dutch soldiers guarding us.

We spent a peaceful Sunday afternoon in a small, solid, Dutch country house with its numerous signs of secure family life. I wondered for how many years, on other such Sunday evenings, its owners had strolled by the lake throwing pieces of good Dutch bread to the glistening swans. Suddenly I wanted to know about the family; who they were and where they had gone, so hastily abandoning the pattern of their smooth lives. Did they know of the onslaught on their private rooms—whose furnishings were instinct with the intimate reminders of family friends and close relations? Did they realize that in their cool woods ugly buses drunkenly leant against the trees—sharply snapping off branches that might be in their way? My questions returned to me unanswered . . . there was no one with the necessary information, and worse, no one who cared.

Night came again, bringing back, as in a bad illness, all the fears of the night before considerably heightened now by their air of faint familiarity. At dusk the house was shuttered, and we were all bidden to go indoors. Planes and bombs were now on the increase and as the night descended we were in almost complete darkness. In the late afternoon we had been given a small meal, and we realized now that food had run out completely. We knew that it had been the last meal possible for us to obtain on Dutch soil; it had cost, anyway, the greater part of my precious £25. Once darkness had fallen the front door was continually opened to admit more and more refugees. The atmosphere was stifling, and it was difficult to find anywhere to sit down. One group of refugees wore pyjama-like convict clothes and their heads were shaven. They were Poles, who had escaped from some German labour camp. They settled themselves in a corner of one room and there in the dark they sang Polish folk-songs—until our frayed nerves unkindly wished them all back from whence they came.

About midnight we were given an order to form into long lines and to hang on to each other's shoulders; we were then told to file out into the night as our group-names were called out. 'Vic-Wells' was a group-name by itself. In our hastily formed and checked smaller groups, 'Vic-Wells' marched out into the dark woods as one long crocodile, with a Dutch soldier in charge. We came to our bus, packed in, and joined on to the rest of the silent convoy. There were no lights: at the head of the convoy was a motor bike with a small headlight and the same at the rear. The surrounding night sounded like fireworks at the Crystal Palace, with the appropriate accompanying flashes in the sky showing through the trees.

We now started on a slow and nerve-racking journey. Stops were frequent; they occurred whenever there was a sharp exchange of fire, either in the skies directly over us or amidst the surrounding woods. When this occurred everyone had to get down on to the floor of the bus to avoid stray bullets, shrapnel, or a possible bomb. Once more the comparative silence would return: then on again through the night at snail's pace, with the fiercely burning fires in the distance angrily illuminating the landscape.

We reached the port of Ymuiden about two hours before daybreak: it must have been approximately two o'clock. A cargo boat awaited us and we were instructed to join the queue of refugees lined up to go on board. The queue stretched down the quayside, like a fat depressing snake, hugging the edge of the quay as if it drew some comfort from getting as close as possible to the dark waters. At the tail end were the refugees from Amsterdam: a monotonous message was relayed, continuously, to those further up the line—'Will some of the men come to the rear and help the Amsterdam folk with their luggage?' No one moved; the reason was obvious; no one else had been allowed to take any luggage with them! In front of me there stood what looked like a small, gloomy British commercial traveller, hunched in his Burberry with his hat pulled well down over his ears; all at once he swung round and, charged with a sudden sense of life, he bawled in reply: 'Tell the folk from Amsterdam to look after their own b—— luggage.' Peace followed this undoubtedly practical suggestion.

But peace was limited to the Amsterdam folk and their luggage: dawn showed faint signs of breaking as we anxiously watched the slow progress of the queue; more anxiously still did our eyes wander to the occasional plane swooping down over the harbour, belching fire at anything it considered worth hitting: our precious cargo boat seemed an easy and tempting target. At last we reached the gangway, where anxious sailors, knowing the boat must sail before daylight, even at the expense of its human freight, hurried us on. 'Vic-Wells this way,' we heard again, and our numbed senses responded: mine though were suddenly crudely alert, for 'this way' was the one way that I most dreaded—we had to descend a single gangway, leading down into the hold of the ship. Down however we all went, and the hold of that ship is a picture that will never fade.

Lit by a few hurricane lamps it held about four hundred people; close together they lay, or sat, on a thick layer of straw that covered the entire flooring. Sanitary arrangements were primitively set up in corners behind rough canvas hangings. At the far end was a rough couch, softly lit by an overhanging lamp, and partly encircled with some canvas draperies . . . on this lay an expectant mother in the charge of two nurses . . . everything was stilled in me for a fleeting moment, for the couch uncannily suggested a manger.

I stood at the foot of the gangway with my group, counting the other groups as they descended. Behind me a monotonous voice kept crying out 'Fred—Fred—Fred', and in a sudden fit of irritation I turned round. My impatience was swiftly transformed into a feeling of deep compassion: for the man crying out so shamelessly on that cruel chaotic night for his lost friend was blind.

The Company settled themselves in the straw in the dimly-lit hold; Frederick Ashton checked each group with me. The congestion was such that it was necessary to walk across outstretched bodies, fumbling for a clear space on which to place one's foot. I lay down, at last, in the new dinner jacket, and Fred handed me two handfuls of straw to make a pillow; I felt like a horse about to be fed.

A hazardous journey started across the North Sea that lasted for fifteen hours. About mid-morning we were allowed up on deck for some fresh air; by then two graceful, silver grey escorting destroyers were making wide patrolling circles around us. Sea breezes though for us did not last long; enemy aircraft were spotted overhead and we were ordered back to the hold.

We reached Harwich just before dark on the evening of that never-to-be-forgotten Whit Monday. Already docked was the ship that brought Queen Wilhelmina and the British Embassy over, and two fussy tugs steamed to and fro between us and the mainland. It was suddenly all over—and we were on shore. Tea and sandwiches were pressed on us by the W.V.S. helpers, and a train waited to take us to London.

We reached the London terminus about 1 a.m. on the Tuesday morning: a silent group of relations and friends met us. The home-coming was quiet.

•   •   •

It took us a few days to be aware of the assault of the Wind in the Clock. England eyed the situation with the controlled anxiety of the head of a large family confronted with a domestic crisis that no care-ful planning could avoid: it was a question of facing up to the blow, and thus gauging the force of the impact; the first move seemed to be the acquisition of a proper sense of perspective, so as to make the return of the blow a possibility at some future date.

The Dutch adventure resulted for the Sadler's Wells Ballet in a crippling loss of properties. Eight of our major ballets, together with the music scores (some in manuscript) and orchestral parts, were locked up in Holland for the duration of the war.

Tyrone Guthrie, the director of Sadler's Wells, applied himself to obtaining some financial compensation from the British Council. A season of ballet was due to open almost directly at Sadler's Wells and so Guthrie, Lambert and myself held long conferences on how we could retrieve our position to the best economic advantage. I had had, for some time, a new ballet in preparation (a work inspired by Rowlandson to music by Boyce arranged by Lambert) bearing the ominous title of *The Prospect Before Us*!

During the interim period, before we could collect ourselves for the London season, the Company was sent on a short E.N.S.A. tour of the Aldershot district. The poor things immediately encountered a night bombing raid at one of the military camps; the attacking planes, aiming at military objectives, merely succeeded in dropping bombs in the garden of the house that the dancers were billeted in: five bombs in a straight line—just missing the roof of the house.

In London we went ahead, preparing feverishly for the season which we eventually managed to present. *Dante Sonata* was given on the first night and the impact was dramatic on the audience for it was danced to the accompaniment of a gramophone record: understandably, Lambert had not had time to re-score the work.

The war news grew steadily worse, and the inevitable fall of France drew ever nearer. I can remember meeting Lord Lloyd (about to leave England for France on a desperate last-minute conference) in the foyer of Sadler's Wells Theatre at a Saturday matinée. 'France,' he said to me quietly, 'will fall—but we shall win—some day.' I was aghast; I went outside the theatre to wander miserably up and down my familiar Islington.

•   •   •

Now all is confusion: France has fallen and all our thoughts are concentrated on the plight of the British Expeditionary Force. It is approaching high summer and life continues its taut yet disjointed round; the result of the general submission to a new automatism that has descended on us and become overnight a habit of long standing.

I find myself sitting in the Wells Room and I am trying to concentrate on the music score of *The Prospect Before Us*. George Chamberlain, our general manager, passes swiftly through the room: he tells me that his son is back from France—for the little boats of our island-home have already started their Dunkirk saga. I feel happy for him, and thanks to his news now await, with more optimism, the return of my elder brother—still, as far as one can know anything, on the beaches of Dunkirk.

We succeeded in producing *The Prospect Before Us* during that summer season at the Wells, and were accorded a first night audience that packed the theatre to the roof. It seemed strange that at such a time our public could rock with merriment at Helpmann's clowning, and could bestow on the ballet such an enthusiastic reception. Looking at that crowded scene of swaying oval heads, pink-fronted as with masks seen indistinctly, everything that was happening elsewhere seemed impossible: but we were living a new life, shaped for the duration of the world's madness; until this thing ended, every action would have about it a tempestuous timelessness, a clock awhirl indeed—with the wind within it rising to a gale.

The Opera and the Ballet were still performing at the Wells when the Battle of Britain began. In those early days, the Home Office decided that, when the air raid alert was given, all entertainment in the theatre would cease for a space of about ten minutes, to enable any member of the audience to leave the theatre if he felt so inclined. At moments the arrangement was not without a touch of grim humour, as, for instance, the night when the alert was given just as the drop scene of *The Prospect Before Us* was lowered in the middle of the ballet. This curtain depicted Rowlandson's eighteenth-century theatre in flames, and the audience of that period in a state of comic panic. In the deadly silence of our theatre, a silence inflicted on us by the stern command of authority, we sat and stared uncomfortably at the bucolic and bawdy painting which spelt Rowlandson to the accompaniment of the barrage and the bombs, busily engaged in shaking the very foundations of London.

This grim method of allowing the public to choose between the possibility of burial within, or extermination without, proved conclusively that the vast majority preferred entertainment above ground to a shelter underground: it is a fact that nobody was ever known to move in search of any form of official safety; so it ended in officialdom accepting defeat, and permitting entertainment to continue with its own answering barrage.

•   •   •

My mind glides backwards; it is, for the moment, checked by the recollection of one summer night.

The evening performance is over, and, to everyone's satisfaction, has been completed without any celestial interruptions. I accompany Frederick Ashton to his charming little Islington house. Dotted about between the prim and spacious early Victorian Squares and the older Regency and eighteenth-century ones, are to be found in this Islington that we know and love, enchanting, small, isolated houses. They are nonchalant erections, with sometimes a tiny garden —symbol of the day when man could choose his way of life, his roof, and his patch of land with but a fleeting regard for the opinion of town planners. Obscurity encircles such houses, and bestows on them a quietude that is born of independence; it so happens that often their modest position makes them immune from the march of progress that causes a symmetrical regiment of their neighbours to suffer destruction to make way for some form of industrial development.

Michael Somes, who lives in the adjoining Lloyd Square, is ahead of us for he has been entrusted with the cooking of the supper; Sophie Fedorovitch makes up our party of four. Why does such a small domestic scene, played out nearly twenty years ago, grip my heart and eye, in a harmony worthy of a discerning draughtsman, bent on making a clear-cut etching of the remembered scene? I think the reason is that at such times a deep humanity, unexpressed by anyone, but felt by all, is present.

Michael is cooking corn-on-the-cob; he twirls with his fingers the pointed green tops; the movement attracts me and I note that it is rapid so as to avoid the steam rising from the fast-boiling water. Sophie sits wrapt in her silent resignation. Suddenly the night is rent by sirens; near and far they ride the skies as witches might, cutting the air with an eerie cry that denotes their gathering speed through space. With the rhythm of the perfected timing of brutality comes the barrage setting up its ceaseless game of ninepins with the bombers. The little house shakes: we all concentrate on the green points sticking up through the steam . . . 'It is nothing,' mumbles Sophie, with closed eyes; her contemptuous bass voice in harmony with her granite-like little figure, symbolizing to us her ravaged Poland. This briefest of monologues was drawn from her as a deafening crash shook the neighbourhood. She voiced what we all felt; the necessity of holding on to energy, sanity and a sense of proportion.

•   •   •

'Nothing,' though, makes its own demands on the pattern of living, and the City's bombed-out families are becoming a problem. Entertainment must give way, must, if necessary, be interrupted, and Sadler's Wells Theatre finds itself commandeered as a refuge for the homeless. Most of the administrative staff are sleeping on the premises in the downstairs dressing-rooms; kitchens are set up in the bars, and the theatre throws its doors open to a new public—the North London population that is temporarily bombed out from the familiar shelter of its crowded tenement houses. Night after night the cockney inhabitants of North London are brought in by indefatigable civil defence workers; they camp in the theatre until the authorities can manage to evacuate or re-house them.

The Opera and Ballet are now homeless and must once more take to the open road; the towns and cities of England, but without orchestras: from now on we tour with two pianos only.

High up though in the Sadler's Wells Theatre, in the large mirror-lined rehearsal room, with its huge glass windows, was still housed the School of Ballet—open from 9 a.m. to 2 p.m. Its doors were only closed for three months in the summer of 'forty-four, when the height of the V-1 bomb menace made it too dangerous a venture. I ran the School for the first two years of the war with Nicolai Ser-gueeff; then, on account of my increasing activities with the Company when Frederick Ashton was called up, Ursula Moreton took my place with the students for a short time; she was followed by Ailne Phillips; later, Vera Volkova replaced Sergueeff.

In that early autumn of 1940 I can see the younger generation at work in the classroom, while the soup kitchens function in the base-ments, and the barrage balloons float outside the windows.

There is the long slim silhouette of Moyra Fraser, just about to be promoted to the Company (having already been taken to Holland as an 'extra' with the added approval of an unsuspecting Bow Street Magistrate). Already her distinctive quality lay in her mimicry, which was the delight of old Sergueeff. He would tell me, with many chuckles (and he had a chuckle that resembled the neighing of a horse) how good her imitation was of June Brae's 'Lilac Fairy'. 'Velly, velly, clever,' he would say, wagging his head in his content-ment.

'Little King' has gone North with her parents, but she will return later, and blaze a trail as Moira Shearer. Thirteen-year-old Beryl Grey (she is still at this stage, 'Miss Groom') disappears for one whole year—evacuated with her school to some small place in the North. Among the younger boys there is John Field, shortly to join the Company until his call-up comes along. A small, fair boy with unbe-lievably long legs comes up twice every week on the milk train from Bournemouth, so as to be at the nine o'clock class. He is twelve years of age, and one day apologizes, solemnly, for being stupid; he then explains that he has been up all night in an air raid shelter, and that he had to stand on the milk train. He is very tired, he adds gravely. The little boy is Philip Chatfield.

As time went on we slowly collected Brian Shaw, Donald Britton

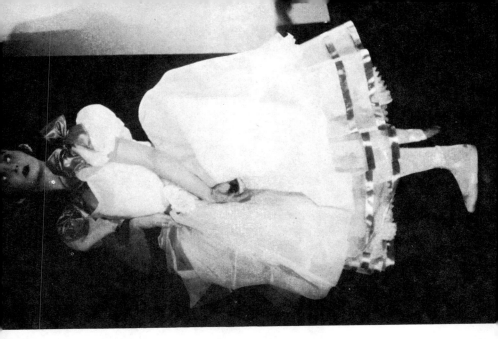

SADLER'S
WELLS ROLES
IN THE
THIRTIES

Left: Swanilda
in 'Coppelia'

*Right: Pas de
Trois* in 'Les
Rendez-Vous'

BRUSSELS,
JANUARY 1945
Left to right:
Moira Shearer,
Alexis Rassine,
Margot Fonteyn,
Douglas Stewart,
Pamela May

PARIS, 1945
Group includes, left to right: Robert Helpmann, Stewart Granger, Moyra Fraser,
Deborah Kerr, Leslie Edwards

and Michael Boulton. Rosemary Lindsay and Anne Heaton were among the very young girls; one or other would sometimes turn up at the New Theatre, to sit on the balcony as the Doll in *Coppélia*.

When we suspended our ballet school in 'forty-four for three months, one little boy was sent North to his home. He panicked at the sudden isolation, and fretted over the lost companionship of his fellow students; so he ran away. His method was to hitch-hike his way across war-scarred England in order to get back to London and the Sadler's Wells School. The police caught him in London, before he had had the chance to communicate with us; they were sceptical about his explanation—for who had ever heard of a small boy running back to any sort of school?

I think that I will pause here and pay a tribute to the wartime parents. Not once during those six, desperate years did I get one letter bewailing the hard work, rough living, and continual danger to which these young people were subjected for the greater part of the period. It is true that the women artists of call-up age were exempted from military service, if they were applied for by their managements for any regular work concerned with the more important forms of cultural entertainment. We had, though, many young artists far too young for any war service—between the ages of 14 and 17. These mere children would wend their way through a London or provincial blackout during periods of continual raids, yet no parent ever bombarded me with letters expressing parental worry. Our students grew up in the theatre in conditions that would seem impossible today; they had encouragement from their homes to stick to their work, and their parents let me see that they had every intention of taking full responsibility for the consequences. This additional example of thoughtfulness struck me as unbelievably reasonable at such a time of strain and stress.

Our small wartime Company was, about this time, strengthened by the addition of Gordon Hamilton from Australia and Alexis

Rassine from South Africa. Rassine's parents were Lithuanians; they had settled in South Africa many years ago. Alexis spoke Russian; he had, though, received his education in South Africa and so he could only write in English. His mother spoke English; but, on account of her Eastern European education, only wrote in Russian . . . so they could not correspond. Alexis Rassine has certain values by which he lives and reasons—the rest goes by him: his is the philosophy of a singularly untheatrical nature. Partnering Nadia Nerina on her debut in *The Sleeping Beauty* in New York (to a packed house and the entire New York press) he said, 'You've nothing to worry about, my dear, Madam's not in front this afternoon.' I once discovered while he was with us that he had gone to Brighton for a whole day with his dog: I inquired if he had spent the day alone—he assured me that he had not, for he had taken a book with him . . .

If ever I stopped to consider the general situation during the war, I found myself longing for some form of complete detachment. Tyrone Guthrie once said to me that he had moments when he longed to become just a part of the war machine—and to be ordered about as such, with all thoughts of individual effort suspended. Many times had I felt the same reaction sweep over me. I thought of the theatre only as a part of the war, and the ballet only as a part of the wartime theatre; then again, both theatre and ballet only as something to be preserved for those that the war machine had temporarily swallowed up. Yet, when at work, it always came down to the perfecting of the detail of a performance, or the interminable struggle of fighting for a good general standard; on such occasions I would cynically reflect that I was not unlike the sergeant teaching the wartime recruit the necessity of tidy puttees, or I was reminded of the pre-war officer who wore mess kit for dinner in a desert tent.

Up and down the country went the Company during that grim autumn and winter of 1940–41. From time to time I would pay them visits, and on one such occasion I arrived in Birmingham in the late afternoon, with the intention of going on the following morning to their E.N.S.A. camp base. On that very night Birmingham received one of its biggest raids. My hotel was opposite the Wren cathedral. Incendiaries hit the flat roof of the cathedral and, burning through, fell with a shower of sparks into the body of the church, while the church windows, lit by the inferno within, looked like illuminated Christmas cards. In the background (on the other side of the square) a huge warehouse, blazing its life out, silhouetted the outline of the church. Still the beautiful tower rose majestically to the skies—unscathed. Patiently, amid the rain of bombs, flashing incendiaries, fierce fires and crashing masonry, the tower clock struck each quarter, each half and each hour throughout the night. Standing there, I found myself echoing Sophie's 'It is nothing': the tower stood like a symbol of contempt against the inferno of the night.

On the pavement beneath the tower firemen swarmed like black ants and with the help of willing civilians trailed their miles of blackened hose that strewed the streets in an imitation of the lines of a great railway terminus.

The next morning saw the blackened walls of the burnt-out church, but the tower was intact—still measuring out the hours of the day.

I left early for the Birmingham suburb where I expected to find the Company, but soon discovered that the raid had been widespread, and that many an innocent outlying district, in no way involved in the war effort, had felt repercussions from the raid on the city. I came at last to the district that I sought and successfully tracked down the house that had been allotted to the Company as their headquarters. My heart then seemed to miss a beat, for the building was a shambles, with the whole of the back blown away. My memory preserves to this day a picture of a sordid tin bath dangling indecently, flaunting its cheap brass taps and its stunted bow legs, from the remnants of a sparsely equipped bathroom. A man standing nearby answered the

question that I did not dare put to him: he told me that if I was looking for the people who had been there for some days, I was wasting
my time; they had been moved on—the morning before the raid.

Gone now for good were the old Sadler's Wells days—gone also
its people, for before Christmas, the Vic-Wells offices and headquarters had been moved to Burnley, in the Midlands, whence it was
easier for the administrative staff to direct the tours of the three
Companies.

When I entered the theatre each morning on my way up to the
School quarters, I would encounter strange black shapes emerging
from its depths. Large, fat, slow old women of Islington would seek
the air that they had breathed since birth. They resembled black
beetles, as they stood discussing, with a certain relish, the happenings
of the night behind them. Pinched, grubby, pale-faced children ran,
played and quarrelled on the wide pavements—keen as their parents
to dodge the welfare officer, bent, understandably, on persuading
these 'died-in-the-wool' Londoners to send their children to the
country. But the true city dwellers (and most of ours were born in
and around Smithfield) mistrust the country. One woman told me
she would never take the kids to the country, for where was there
for a body to hide in a field?

By the New Year the Home Office manifested the wish that the
theatres in London should endeavour to provide some distraction for
the public. A policy of giving, first, matinées, and then very early
evening performances (as the days lengthened) was formed.

On a morning following one of London's worst raids—the raid
that left St. Paul's standing midst a bedlam of smoke, water, and fire
that lasted throughout the following day—I came up to London to
see Sir Bronson Albery, managing director of the New Theatre and
a Governor of the Old Vic and Sadler's Wells.

I had first been to the School: then had to make my way from
Islington to St. Martin's Lane on foot, for the chaos of the night had

left its marks for miles around—like a spent and panting beast. Fire engines were still returning from the City after their night and morning fight, their crews as black as crows with the smoke, their faces shining with the sweat of the heat and toil of the night—defying even the cold of this bitter January morning. At last I reached the New Theatre, and spent the early afternoon with Sir Bronson and his son Donald. This theatre was about to try the experiment of taking on the ballet and the opera for alternate seasons of eight weeks, which would break up the endless touring, and contribute something to the renewal of London theatre life.

We played matinées only for our first season: such an arrangement gave people time to get home before the raids started; by the summer, though, the raids began so late in the evening that it was possible to reinstate early evening performances. We were, of course, still limited to the use of two pianos.

During the spring I worked on a ballet to Gluck's *Orpheus* with Sophie Fedorovitch, who came and stayed with me at Sunningdale, armed with her paints, her brushes, and her tranquillity. The Company returned to London in the early summer for a lengthy season at the New Theatre.

The general tight-rope existence continued, but at least one knew that even the government recognized the intense necessity of the theatre in the life of the people. Anxiety and difficulty continued of course: going home to Sunningdale on those summer nights, I would see, from the window of my train, a raid start on London. It meant that one's thoughts would be occupied with the safety of the Company and one's personal friends—coupled with the hope that our theatre would be standing the next day, for it housed all our hard-earned belongings; by now, we had replaced about two-thirds of the ballets lost in Holland, and were also slowly adding new works suitable for presentation under present conditions.

That summer saw the call-up of the last of all our senior male dancers. Ashton, even, was in the R.A.F. by August. The entertainment world greatly needed us, but it was an increasing struggle to keep up any real standard. We took boys of sixteen, straight from the School and elsewhere, into the Company, and were thus able to get two years' work out of them before their call-up.

The September of '41 brought a complete change of fortune to the theatre. The great boom had set in that was to last from '42 until some time after the war. Thanks to the exodus from London of residents, as well as government officials, provincial theatres were packed, both in the cities and the smaller towns. During these years raids were spasmodic—heavy during the long winter nights, but dying away altogether for a period of about fifteen months.

The Company worked very hard during those years: they were permitted two weeks' annual holiday and for every eight weeks spent in London a corresponding eight weeks must be spent in the provinces. But how our public grew! Everyone on war work went to the theatre, and a vast, young public was ours, for children, up and down the country, were brought to the ballet as a means of bringing some light and relief into their small, disturbed and broken-up lives. At one time the demand for tickets on the part of London war workers was so great that we were compelled to give three performances on Saturdays.

·   ·   ·

I must now go back to the late summer of 1941.

With signs of the boom on the horizon I was determined to revive *The Sleeping Beauty*; for this ballet had not been given since the war had started. I had a prolonged luncheon, at the Ivy Restaurant, with Sir Bronson Albery, Tyrone Guthrie and George Chamberlain, Sadler's Wells General Manager. I wanted to persuade them to take the plunge and reinstate the orchestra. Mr. Chamberlain had come armed with a set of figures showing very clearly that we were doing steady business with the two pianos; he then showed the loss we should incur on such takings if we burdened ourselves with an orchestra. My challenge was to present another set of figures showing what I thought the orchestra would do for us, first as a financial asset in itself, and secondly as a financial asset by permitting the reinstatement of the classical ballets which we could not give without an orchestra. My figures were, of course, based on supposition only —Mr. Chamberlain's on facts. So no male moved . . . however, somehow a compromise was reached as follows: Mr. Guthrie said I could have an orchestra for two weeks if the Vic-Wells Association would back it financially. I, on my part, guaranteed to revive *The Sleeping Beauty*. Guthrie would not allow the finances of the theatre to back those two weeks—he feared the possible loss of money; he was not prepared to take the risk with the burden of the two theatres on his hands. (The Old Vic had been badly bombed and Sadler's Wells was, from every angle, except that of the school, out for the duration of the war.) The Vic-Wells Association came to our rescue; I plunged at *The Sleeping Beauty*, though so youthful were some of the cast that in places it resembled a kindergarten romp rather than a ballet. It put, however, Fonteyn back at the head of the kind of ballet that she needed for her full development; it gave the audience and the dancers the uplift from the orchestra pit for which they had longed; it placed Mr. Lambert once more on the rostrum; best of all it packed the theatre night after night, for we turned people away by the hundreds.

Mr. Guthrie's nerve returned: we were never again without an orchestra and gradually all the classics were reinstated. At a later date *Le Lac des Cygnes* was actually remounted, on sumptuous lines, by Leslie Hurry, following his successful production of *Hamlet* with Robert Helpmann.

•   •   •

A haze descends: I see through it many faces and places, in changed circumstances but all stamped with the hallmark of this particular period in our history.

In my forty-fourth year my age-group was called up. I was in the North with the Ballet and went to register there. A woman, wearing the expression of someone bidden to sit on one ice-block, and lean back against another, rapped out her questions. In one minute she had discovered many things: that I was married; that my husband was a busy doctor; that the surgery was a part of our private house; that the Ministry of Labour allowed us one maid; that I was employed by the Governors of Sadler's Wells as director of the Ballet; that I had to go home every week-end to attend to the duties of a doctor's house and let my maid have the Sunday off. She then asked if I had any children, and as the answer was in the negative, announced, with enormous finality, that I came under the category of no responsibilities. The tip of her long, masterful pencil pointed to the printed question 'Have you any responsibilities?' With arctic politeness she instructed me to write 'None'. I did so. She was a happy woman. She then informed me, with an icy smile, that I would receive further instructions in due course. The lady's threat of 'instructions in due course' never materialized: something about my activities must have filled some bureaucratic breast with sympathy: no further duplication, confirmation or inquiry was required. I was left to continue my carefree existence.

Bloomsbury Square was still part of my life, with the architectural beauties of its surrounding districts much damaged. I paid my occasional visit to No. 46, for Keynes and his wife remained in London. His work at the Treasury necessitated this arrangement, in spite of his health which always gave cause for anxiety. Life at forty-six was changed from the now nostalgic '30s. The friendly, spacious drawing-room of the past, scattered with books and periodicals, its long windows elegantly curtained and its walls covered with the choicest of Maynard's collection of paintings, was closed. The Keynes lived on the ground floor, dining in the basement kitchen and hanging on its walls the art treasures from the drawing-room. They led a quiet existence, amidst their domestic restrictions, taking life and the war very philosophically.

Lydia was indefatigable in her protection of Maynard from the minor irritations of the day, knowing that she was helpless against his vast major duties. She accepted the fact that his country had need of his genius to unravel many problems. She had the Russian capacity for countering reverse of fortune with action or an expression of disarming frankness. (In her dancing days she would never say that a certain rôle had not suited her—she would announce, 'I was a flop . . . it had to stop.') She accompanied Maynard to Washington on his two all-important visits. She went to the States in the same clothes that she wore in bomb-scarred Bloomsbury, her head wrapped in a scarf which was, more often than not, replaced by an expensive pre-war silk stocking. She told me, after her first visit, that there were wonderful things to buy in Washington, but that she was only able to afford two blouses, because, as she said, 'I am Treasury, and I must have ethics.' Her solicitude for Maynard could, in the interests of his health, lead Lydia to take a firm line. At the beginning of the war I visited them early one morning as I had heard that he was ill and had been ordered a week's rest; Lydia greeted me in the hall looking rather stern and pained—and told me to go straight in to Maynard's room. I found him sitting up in bed, surrounded with large pillows and looking quietly guilty. 'Lydia is upset,' he informed me gravely. 'You see, this morning she discovered that I had written to *The Times*. . . .'

There was a week at Oxford when I decided that, as the Company was going on to Bath for the following week, I would break with my usual habit of returning to London for the week-end and go on instead to Bath—a city that I dearly loved to stay in. However it was not to be, for I was called back to London on Saturday morning on business. On the Sunday morning, there was a strong rumour that Bath had been bombed; on the Monday I caught an early train to rejoin the Company, travelling with Donald Albery, who was now our general manager. Just as we were about to leave, a porter announced that he did not know when we would get to Bath; communications with the city were almost impossible, as they had had a second bad raid on the Sunday night. I shall never forget the suspense of that journey, for, of course, the whole Company (eighty strong with the orchestra) had been in that small city that night.

When we got to Bath the city looked like a cracked bowl; along the streets were queues of people, many still in their night attire, waiting for transport to take them to relief centres. Mobile breakfast vans trundled about, feeding them; there was water and smoke everywhere, and widespread damage. But the Company was intact and no one was hurt. They had been housed all over the town in lodgings, boarding houses and hotels: in the circumstances it was a miracle that they all survived unhurt. Jean Bedells and three other young girls had been given a shake-down in the theatre (their lodgings had not survived the Saturday night raid). The theatre was hit the night that they were sleeping there—and quite a lot of it completely burnt out.

Out of curiosity I went to see the hotel that I should have stayed in on the Saturday: only one-third of it was standing: it had received a direct hit in the Saturday night raid.

We appeared to be heading for another Holland: Monday morning disclosed that our ballets were shut up in trucks on a siding at Bath station; it also revealed that a couple of time bombs were sitting on the rails in the close vicinity of the trucks. Nothing could be done: either the bombs would go off, or they might prove themselves to be duds and remain silent, or they might again be skilfully removed by the demolition squad. Meanwhile the trucks sat there for several days: I forget the ultimate fate of the bombs—but our trucks at least were not blown up.

It is the summer of '44, and through the haze something is now discernible. As a start, the Fates chose my birthday for D-Day: thus time wiped out, in no uncertain manner, the indignity of the dismantled bonfire.

On the night of 16th June I decided to stay in London, the guest of Eveleigh Leith (our wartime press representative) in her little house in Walton Street. Raids had been spasmodic, with periods of quite lengthy calm. We had gone to bed when we heard the alert and the follow-up of the barrage. Suddenly a plane seemed to skim the top of the house, and a minute later there was a loud explosion. I decided that it would teach them not to fly so low, and settled down to sleep. In ten minutes there was another plane, just as low, and travelling in the same direction: within seconds came another loud explosion. I got out of bed and went to the window: some distance away, following another line of flight. I saw a curious, low-lying plane, flying over the rooftops; a glow of fire came from its tail; it disappeared, and after a minute there was another of these now familiar explosions. The hours wore on through this extraordinary night, filled with giant-sized fireflies rushing across the sky with their tails aglow. Then it was morning, with a heavy, overcast sky; the all-clear had never sounded; the new fireflies continued unabated, though hidden now by low-lying clouds, and the explosions did not cease. I went back to the theatre midst the wondering population bent on its day's work; faces appeared bewildered; a little fretful to find that there was something fresh to keep them awake at night and harass them all day.

Later in the morning we were given to understand that Hitler's V-1 had arrived.

Throughout the summer season at the New Theatre we experienced by far the most tiresome situation of the war; an over-rich savoury to wind up a wartime dinner of many and varied courses. The old-fashioned raids were a thing of the past, looked back on almost with affection; in retrospect they seemed to wear a certain dignity and allow of some respite when compared with the noisy mosquito of this summer arriving every ten or fifteen minutes. It was odd, though, how people found the instructions given to ensure a certain element of safety, too self-conscious-making to carry out. I can remember solemnly informing the Company, at rehearsal on the stage of the New Theatre, that when they heard the engine stop, they must fling themselves on the ground, as the explosion followed after a count of ten. Some eight minutes later one of these fiends passed over us: the engine stopped: everyone stood still and counted ten—but no one fell to the ground!

The Company was now suffering badly from lack of sleep; I could sense a very real fatigue, due mostly to bad nights, disturbed days and lack of proper nourishment. These teenagers had had five years of life as dictated by the war; two-thirds of them in the most difficult years of their adolescence and general development. It was taking toll of everyone's reserves and even the reserves of youth were fully taxed. In my opinion it was harder for the young; in the broken home-life due to war conditions they lost their much-needed security; in the bad food, energy for their growing bodies; in their restless nights, sleep that youth cannot forego so easily as the adult.

The London season came to an end and we were once more headed for the provinces; it was to be our last season for some time, at the New Theatre, for it had been decided that as the Old Vic Company, now under the leadership of Laurence Olivier and Ralph Richardson, was to have a season in St. Martin's Lane, we should appear in the early autumn at the Prince's Theatre.

A rumour is abroad; a rumour that fills our tour-weary Company with renewed zeal and interest in life. I am summoned to London to discuss the details of a plan, proposed by E.N.S.A., to send us overseas to Europe the following January. It is to be a tour of Belgium and France (mainly Brussels and Paris) complete with orchestra; in Basil Dean's estimation it is to be the biggest theatrical contingent ever to appear in a garrison theatre, and we are to take with us all the necessary scenery and costumes.

We returned to London for our autumn season at the Prince's Theatre, where we produced Helpmann's second ballet: *Miracle in the Gorbals*. The success was immense and we played to capacity houses for several weeks.

One night, during a performance, I was leaving the stage door; suddenly there was a shattering explosion quite near—then the usual fire-engine and signs of disaster in the vicinity. There was no alert, no all-clear; only again, a little later, another such deafening noise and the sound of crumbling masonry . . . we now knew that death and damage were to strike, indiscriminately, anywhere. It was the night of the V-2's first visit to London. We heard that Hitler's last throw, the V-3, would be the worst of the lot. Happily for us it never materialized—but V-1 and V-2 made themselves felt until the spring of 1945.

*   *   *

Our last wartime Christmas is over: we have been fitted for our E.N.S.A. uniform, inoculated, vaccinated, received our passports and are all set for embarkation at Tilbury during the first week in the January of 1945 to leave for a ten weeks' tour of Belgium and France. We are to open in Brussels.

The idea of seeing another country, after five years of the round of London and the provinces, was like being let out of a trap.

The winter itself was bitter, with a great deal of snow on the ground; our troopship was a crowded affair, with nine women in a cabin for four (five had to sleep on the floor) and the men swinging in hammocks somewhere below deck. Our spirits, though, were high—in spite of the first sight of ravaged Ostend in the cold light of an early winter morning.

Our train journey to Brussels took fifteen hours; we did not arrive until after midnight, having spent the last part of the journey in a blacked-out train, with no heating and much scarcity of window pane.

We were billeted in a huge military hotel and were to see at close sight the plight of a liberated capital. Gas and electricity for any form of light, heat and hot water concerned with domestic needs were non-existent from 7 a.m. to 7 p.m. Hurricane lamps lit the hotel stairs, set on the floor in corners, for the lifts did not work during the greater part of the twenty-four hours. Outside there were four inches of snow on the ground. The population suffered great privations, and one of the most heart-rending sights was to see very small children armed with tiny bags, following a military coal-wagon: they would creep under it and collect any small pieces of coal that might fall out of the sacks during delivery.

We were well fed, on American tinned foodstuffs, which we found delicious and varied after our English rations. The black market left us aghast; first, that it could exist, with so much hardship in evidence, and second that it was so open an affair; plenty of restaurants would serve anything, at a price.

The Ballet appeared in a large theatre, where an English or American soldier was allowed to bring one Belgian civilian with him to the performance. Each night five hundred seats were kept in reserve for men on forty-eight hours' leave from the battlefields. Long khaki queues formed themselves down the street; many of our present-day audience became interested in the ballet when they first saw us in the Brussels garrison theatre in that January of 1945.

The cold in the theatre was frightful: shivering 'Sylphides' stood in their orderly lines, arousing both appreciation and sympathy from the muffled-up khaki audience. Our staff and wardrobe had to work throughout the night, on account of gas and electric light restrictions. They would return to the hotel at 7 a.m. when we were once more subjected to every sort of cut in the supply of heat and light.

The inevitable heavy outbreak of 'flu swept through the Company, but nothing could damp our spirits; we were having a wonderful time and the discomforts of life seemed of no importance. I visited, on my evening 'flu round, Moira Shearer, who was one of the victims. She was sitting up in bed, and by her side was a bottle of champagne. It had been sent up to her by an officer staying in the hotel, whom she did not know, but who had heard that she was ill. I asked her what she was going to do. 'I can't do anything really, madam,' says Moira gaily, 'you see we have drunk it all.' Moira was, at that time, quite a humble member of the Company, but her beauty, even when in the *corps de ballet*, caused a sensation among the public. She showed character, and a very level head: I was puzzled when she would continually refuse to go to small parties. She gave her explanation, when pressed, to Joy Newton, the ballet mistress. 'First they ask Madam and the principals, and then they say they would like to have the Girl with the Red Hair—and I'm not going out as "the Girl with the Red Hair" . . .' She was right; she wished to win through on the merit of her work and her position in the Company, and so, in her eighteenth year, Moira would return to the hostel, night after night, with the younger members of the Company, unless the party (as, of course, was often the case) included everyone.

It was hard to realize that the war was continuing its course some seventy miles away . . . it was, though, brought home to me one day. A boy in the Company developed severe gastric 'flu, and had to be removed to the American Military Hospital as we were about to depart for Paris. I took him there in a Red Cross ambulance. When we reached the hospital we had a long wait in the casualty clearing department and during that wait a convoy of wounded men arrived from a field-hospital. It was a shock to see these men unloaded and laid out on all the available space on the floor and bench: sitting, standing, and lying on stretchers. It jerked me severely back to the madness of life at that moment, holding every facet of emotion up to your eyes like a series of magic mirrors; showing a diversity of pictures that a whole long lifetime might not, in a different page of history, ever have encountered.

Before we left Brussels, the British Council arranged with the E.N.S.A. authorities that we should give two Sunday evening performances for the ordinary civilian population in the Monnaie Theatre—the Brussels State Opera House. They were exciting performances, packed to the doors and most rapturously received by a public starved so long of any contact with the outside world.

Brussels was full of interesting wartime characters; underneath the stage of our garrison theatre there a Resistance news-sheet had been printed, by the Belgian underground movement. The garrison theatre had been run by the Germans for the German troops; it was considered safer to do such things right under the Teutonic nose, a nose notorious for taking the obvious line of looking further afield for trouble. These Belgians played-up their invaders' slower wits to the full: the sheets, when printed, were delivered by a lively old man; one of the scene-shifters. He would place them nonchalantly in the basket of his bicycle, covering them with the German-sponsored paper, and any ration of food that he might have. No German dreamt that any man would risk his life in such an obvious way as to carry his own death warrant on the handlebars of his bicycle: although the basket was often glanced at casually, it was never properly searched. . . . Then there was the famous Golden Cockerel restaurant, where we all dined one night. The proprietor and his wife were the chief means by which British airmen, brought down or parachuted over Belgium, got out of the country along a well-organized escape route. If the little restaurant was full of Germans, the cockerel (in the window) faced one way—if the situation was all clear it faced the other. The men would be kept upstairs until a get-away was possible. For five years these two stolid Belgians, to keep suspicion from themselves, played special rôles. The man pretended to be a stupid drunk, never really sober, or coherent, and unable to give a straight answer to anyone. His wife was said to be an embittered shrew, of rather unpleasant character. They acted their parts to perfection, and were regarded by the German troops in the city as a couple of harmless, minor menaces, with a decent little restaurant. Once only did a couple of disagreeable German soldiers say that they would like to search the top rooms. At that moment, three of our airmen were in hiding upstairs. Only one thing was left to do, and the woman did it. She nagged and begged them to go up and look for themselves and stop insulting her: the Germans got irritated, told her to leave them alone; said they were not interested in her house, and bade her be quick and bring their dinner. Reluctantly she obeyed, grumbling at their refusal to search her house. . . .

I dined one night with a charming English woman married to a

ALEC SHERMAN AND JOY NEWTON

ROBERT HELPMANN, MOYRA FRASER AND
LESLIE EDWARDS

THE AUTHOR IN 1945

Photo by Gordon Anthony

FRENCH AND
ENGLISH
ARTISTS AT THE
PARIS HOME
OF PRINCESS
RADZIWILL-
TUEDE

Group includes:
Roland Petit,
Renée Jeanmaire,
Boris Kochine,
Christian Bérard,
Georges Auric,
Henri Saguet,
Yvette Chauviré
and members of
the Sadler's Wells
Ballet

Belgian. She had written to me and asked me if I would visit her, for she had once been a professional ballroom dancer and much wanted news of England. I dined in some Belgian suburb in a small house, and discovered that, here again, she and her husband had been ardent workers for the Resistance. She said it was fairly safe so long as you took no one into your confidence; not even her husband's parents, who lived a few doors beyond them were told of their son's and daughter-in-law's activities. Again it was British airmen that they sheltered. They were very brave; sometimes these men had to be kept in the small top attic of their house for many weeks; the Belgian husband would take them out, after dark, for short walks. The English woman would sit in the house, knowing that if they did not return, she could not say or do anything, and knowing also that there was always the chance that she might not see any of them again.

Our month in Brussels at last came to an end; it had been full of life and colour and the Company had made many friends. We left by night train for Paris, another long-drawn-out journey in circumstances exactly similar to our trip from Ostend to Brussels.

Something electric seemed to happen to us all at the first sight of Paris after six years. We drove through the streets in an army lorry, early in the morning, and I can still see Margot Fonteyn's expression of sheer happiness at the sight of a city that she had loved so much before the war: in those halcyon days, it had been usual for young dancers to go over and study in the Russian studios in Paris during the long summer vacation.

The Paris season was at the Marigny Theatre and was mainly for U.S.A. servicemen and women. The number of English and American troops in Paris made it impossible for any civilians to enter the theatre. The greatest disappointment was felt by the Paris Opera Ballet; I tried hard to get the military authorities to relax the rule in the case of the French National Ballet, but failed miserably to obtain permission. One evening I was aware that a large party of young E.N.S.A. uniformed artists were in front: I took little heed for a

12

moment, as there were so many plays and concert parties in Belgium and France at that time. Suddenly I had quite another impression: I hastened round to inspect our dressing-rooms and found the artists very intent on their make-up and general preparation for the show; I noted, though, that in no dressing-room was there visible a single E.N.S.A. uniform. . . . Comment, I decided, was outside my office: problems sometimes arise that may be better solved if left to the initiative of those most whole-heartedly concerned: along such lines a way out had been found that made it possible for the Ballet of the Paris Opera to see the English Ballet.

The British Council then arranged for us to give civilian performances, this time in the form of a ten-day season at the Champs-Elysées Theatre. We started quietly enough for the first two performances; after that for the remainder of the season it was quite impossible to get seats. Hundreds of the French public were disappointed; we had a very interesting press, and the season, if it had not been for further commitments with E.N.S.A., could have been greatly extended.

Paris in 1945 had no buses or taxis, owing to the petrol shortage. Heating and lighting were in the same sorry state as in Brussels; food was extremely scarce, but there again the black market flourished. People wore their outdoor clothes in the house; I can recollect visiting French friends and finding their children playing in an icy room, muffled up with scarves and wearing warm boots and woollen gloves. The most valuable present that one could give would be a cake of soap: although, of course, it was rationed in England, it was non-existent in France. Cold cream was also a major gift, for they had none. The artists in the theatre removed make-up with a form of monkey-brand soap, which was all that they could get for any washing purpose. Three cigarettes was a handsome tip, for they fetched big prices on the black market.

I resumed my friendship with Boris Kochno, who used to be Diaghilev's assistant. At the time, he was trying to launch a young company of French dancers, and he asked me to come to a dress rehearsal. I saw that morning the work of a new, young, French choreographer, and was filled with admiration for his talents. The young man was Roland Petit, preparing for his first onslaught on Paris. He seemed to me to be a great deal in advance of any young choreographer in England at that moment, and it appeared certain that he would make a big impression in the immediate post-war period.

On our way back from a tour that stands out in bright colours for all time, we visited Ghent, Bruges and Ostend. I think that we had now collected permanently a vast public made up of Service people who had seen us for the first time in Belgium and in France. We had also laid the foundation stone of our future American public. The Marigny Theatre in Paris was almost exclusively for the Americans, and the English Ballet made a very deep impression on them during the four weeks when U.S.A. servicemen and women packed the French theatre night after night.

.   .   .

It is spring and we are once more back at the New Theatre. It is to be our last season, and is to last for about ten weeks. In the late summer we are to return to Sadler's Wells, prior to a further E.N.S.A. tour of Germany in the latter part of the autumn.

Summer, and we reach the end of the war. The clock stops suddenly; its mad whirl of reckless, feckless time-keeping is over, for the wind has at last gone out of it. There is much to reckon with: the clock of the world must now be wound again by hand, and the hand is seeking for a new key that will fit the mechanism, bringing the clock back to the regularity of the hour, the minute and the second.

I am confronted with my own particular clock, which has kept some sort of time over the years: what sort of key will wind it properly now?

Within me grows the fear that the key of the past will no longer be the right one . . .

•   •   •

The end of a war resembles the end of an unfortunate love-affair. Everything must be obliterated: first the love-affair itself insists on being forgotten, and second the upheaval it has caused makes life, as lived previously, out of the question.

Sadler's Wells Ballet came out of the war possessed of a comfortable sum of money in the bank; and that after paying its half-share of the building debt which, in 1939, was crippling the Sadler's Wells Theatre. The Governors invested a great part of our surplus war-time profits in the Barons Court School buildings, which we were to open at once, as a new branch of the old School, but with this difference, that it would now include general education for the junior students.

Many times during the war I had said that at the close of hostilities we should have to make every effort to get the Company out of the country for some considerable time; understandably (it seemed to me) everyone would be tired of the sight of us; our public would long to welcome back the Russian Ballet Companies, which they had lost to America at the beginning of the war. Their interest, again, would further be aroused by the American Ballet Companies which had made great progress during the war years and would surely visit Europe as soon as it was possible for them to make the voyage.

We did not realize, however, that years of post-war rationing would be necessary and we understood little of the serious state of transport. In brief, we now discovered that no one could get into the country any more than any one could get out.

C.E.M.A.'s wartime work, under the chairmanship of Maynard Keynes, was slowly turning into a project for the protection of the arts in general, under the name of the Arts Council. There was an important move afoot to open the Covent Garden Opera House, and it was considered possible to do this by 1946 if the Sadler's Wells Ballet could be transferred to this new home.

My Governors were, understandably, divided. Some were willing for us to go to Covent Garden if the Opera could go with us, others thought that our place was at Sadler's Wells. I knew that we had outgrown the Sadler's Wells theatre in size; that we were ripe, at this very moment, for further expansion. Everyone knew that the immediate expansion of the ballet was an easier matter than the expansion of the Opera; there was also every proof that the war had already given us a certain international reputation, and that this only needed the encouragement of expansion to turn our efforts into a National Ballet of the right dimensions.

The English National Ballet of today, and tomorrow, should realize that I am trying to express, with great inadequacy, the generous, realistic as well as idealistic, thinking that our Chairman, the late Lord Lytton, and his fellow Governors gave to this matter in the summer and autumn of 1945. In the end they decided to present us to Covent Garden, in the interest of the development of the ballet as a whole. We were the fruits of ten years' pioneer work, and this decision meant that it would become possible for us to develop along lines that would not be possible, on account of its dimensions, in the Sadler's Wells Theatre. The Governors were right of course; and history has shown that this action alone will always stand as an example of the importance of the Islington Theatre.

The change meant, not only the opening of the established Company at Covent Garden, but the planning of the second company and the reorganizing of the School. We aimed at forming, with the two Companies and the School, a unit that would one day stand as a corner stone of the future in this particular branch of the English theatre.

We had come through the war with about three or four new, creative works of importance out of the seven or eight that had been produced during those difficult years. Now though, we had to feed two companies and rehabilitate our scattered male dancers, of whom some had been in the forces for as long as five years. The younger

ones just up from the School could not help out for very long; they
had their own call-up close on their heels.

I think we were borne up by the sheer excitement, the exhilarating
fight ahead—something that challenged our wartime efforts to the
hilt. Could we accept this new responsibility? Could we find a second
wind that would carry us forward to achieve the more exacting
standards that the post-war public would demand of us? As far as I
could see, there was one great danger. I became acutely aware that
our creative energies would have to be more diffused. An Opera
House in the centre of the Metropolis posed different problems to our
life in Islington. It did not necessarily mean that ballets would be—
aesthetically—any better; it meant, though, that the fundamental
conception, in every direction, would necessarily be on a scale
as yet never contemplated. I visualized the possibility of a sudden
weakening—a position akin to that of an army, its lines stretched
to a point where a break through could be effected almost anywhere . . .

The opening was to be in the February of 1946. Once matters
were settled, I had less than six months to prepare for this big change.
I was thus to go back, once more, to one side of the market, the side
that I had for over thirty years so often briefly visited. . . .

It was a great theatre haunted by the shades of exotic Russian
Ballet: it was a theatre that had formed the habit of graciously opening its doors for the summer season, in the manner of some great
hostess opening her town mansion. We were setting out on the
adventure of making this building extend its hospitality to us
throughout the year, challenging it, at the beginning, with nothing
more than a bedraggled, war-weary Company. It could be likened
to a crazy nightmare, wherein I might be given Buckingham Palace,
a few dusters, and told to get on with the spring cleaning. . . .

•   •   •

I had once found *The Sleeping Beauty* in far-off Dublin; it was the
key that unlocked the first theatre door for me. She was wondrously

beautiful as I have already said, and her beauty had haunted my childhood. . . .

Sadler's Wells Theatre had quietly, on a modest scale, brought her to life in 1938. Soon she had to sleep again for two ugly years; then she awoke in war-scarred London, still an economical little Princess, surrounded by her frugal court. Why not dress her up now, and present her as a royal débutante? Had not her first coming-out party been a small affair—a concession to the hard times through which her country was living?

We had a beautiful Princess to awaken with our new court: Margot Fonteyn had once taken a long journey; it had started in far-off Shanghai, many years ago, with Islington as the goal. She would awaken at last, in a sumptuous court: fitting reward for years of regal patience in adversity.

I shall always feel the tempi of the preparation for that reopening of the Royal Opera House with the Sadler's Wells Ballet in the February of 1946. Vividly I see the huge theatre, one morning, its stalls still covered by the smooth wartime ballroom floor, stretching across the great stage itself, complete with a jazz bandstand at each end.

The Opera House became our Lilac Fairy. She waved her wand and the stalls reappeared: red silk chairs were coaxed up from the dirty rabbit warren of storage under the stage. The wand waved again and the stage reappeared; the great orchestra pit, the boxes; rats, dust, dirt could not withstand the challenge—they fled.

Yet Carabosse was there as well; she held sway over coupons for silks and satins, courtly leather boots, and elegant gloves. She saw to it that canvas was bad; and paint, except for camouflage, almost worse. When it came to artificial flowers for garlands and for wreaths she was triumphant, for she had caused such things to disappear at the time when her sway exiled all beauty from the land.

The Lilac Fairy, though, knew where everything was hidden; she had watched over her sleeping kingdom knowing that one day it would once again be hers and now the day had arrived. . . .

To get the vast production going involved numerous compartments working at one and the same time, moving themselves into various workrooms as fast as the rooms could be opened up. Oliver Messel's lovely designs set us, with our restrictions, many a problem. He himself worked as hard as the smallest seamstress. Time flew by, and the only way to check on progress was for me to hold a weekly meeting round the largest table we could find in the theatre, and get a report then and there from the head of every department.

The boys were returning from the forces: Ashton was out just about Christmas time; at about the same time Michael Somes was released from the warlike occupation of breaking up fallen masonry in the bombed areas. Jack Hart returned from Australia; Claude Newman and Richard Ellis from the Navy; Alan Carter from the East; John Field from Belgium. While awaiting demobilisation they turned up at the theatre in uniform and army boots—getting down to a little practice and rehearsal, even before they had actually received their discharge papers. Constant Lambert was, naturally, in his element. For the first time the great Tchaikovsky score would have its seventy players; for the first time, night after night, the traditional two eighteenth-century powdered footmen would close and part those great gold and crimson curtains for an English Ballet.

•   •   •

On 19th February, 1946, up to the moment of the rise of the curtain, in the tradition of the true theatre, the last stitches were being put into the new costumes, the final flower sewn on the fairies' costumes: all was turmoil behind and curiosity in front.

It was a gala that smelt bravely of mothballs: perhaps the first occasion that made post-war London shake out its evening apparel of 1939. I donned the evening dress that I had not left in Holland, and I presume Frederick Ashton was resplendent in the dinner jacket that I slept in on the straw of the cargo-boat hold. . . .

Our gala was graced with the presence of the entire Royal Family and the full Cabinet, yet, viewed in retrospect, almost any first night (and most certainly any opening or closing night of a season today) is more of a gala than that occasion of our opening after the war. The public was divided into those who thought the whole idea preposterous, those who were mildly anxious, and those who had a presentiment that we would, as they put it, get away with it. I was severely criticized in many quarters for attempting anything without calling upon the help of a good number of foreign artists; this, in particular, with reference to the male dancers. Tedious I find it, when people give lengthy explanations of the why and the wherefore: time has spoken for me, and in a kindly, generous fashion. People (other people) have a right to be concerned if they wish, with the part before the whole, and I do not quarrel with them for doing so: I only make my obeisance to the Covent Garden Board and the Administrator (Mr. David Webster) for letting me, once more in my life, in my Turgenev fashion, embark on 'The Longest Way'.

We have arrived now at the final phase of the establishment of a National Ballet. It seems that this particular section ends here on the note of that evening's hesitant, decorous occasion. I can see the stage; I can see, during an interval, the reception room at the back of the Royal Box: I am standing talking, answering the kindly questions of King George VI and the Queen. I find myself in conversation with Queen Mary about Hanover, where I had been, in the autumn, with the Company on an E.N.S.A. tour. The two young Princesses stand out so clearly; particularly I can recall fifteen-year-old Princess Margaret's concern because someone had hinted that Margot Fonteyn's third act costume was not yet finished! Behind it all I wonder what is really happening . . . will our sin be forgiven us, will we expand ourselves sufficiently to fill out our new outsize costume? It is not the interest, the kindly encouragement and understanding of the members of the Royal Box that will be my answer: it will be found tomorrow in the papers; in the days to come in the box office.

Tomorrow came and all was well. Within three days we knew that every seat, for every performance (seven in the week) of *The*

Sleeping Beauty was sold for the full month's run of this ballet. We waited, with some misgivings, for what would happen when we advertised our first programmes of triple bills—three short ballets in one evening which were to be the main fare for the second month.

When the time came the queues at the box office appeared, to my reeling senses, to be longer than ever. . . .

VI

ONE SIDE OF THE MARKET

'Our principal London pleasure was the play, to which we went frequently, generally to Covent Garden, which we soon learned to consider as more decidedly *our* house. We had the Duke of Bedford's private box, sometimes meeting the Duchess of Gordon there, which we liked above all things, for then we had ices, fruits, and cakes in the little ante-room adjoining.'

ELIZABETH GRANT, *Memoirs of a Highland Lady* (1805)

ELIZABETH GRANT was my great-grandmother. Her visits to Covent Garden were made in the year 1805, when she was about eight years old. She met with a certain acclaim for her *Memoirs of a Highland Lady*, written first as a girl in her Highland home, and later when living in London (Lincoln's Inn), Oxford and India. The memoirs end with her marriage in 1830 to General Smith, who owned Baltiboys, the home that my mother, who was the only child of the old lady's son, eventually inherited.

One hundred and fifty years later Elizabeth Grant's great-granddaughter was to sit in the present ante-room of the Duke of Bedford's box; though not to eat cakes with stray Duchesses during a performance dominated by the great Siddons. The great-granddaughter sat there to listen to a new ballet score played on an upright piano that now fills half the rebuilt ante-room, today bereft of elegant chairs and tables adorned with sweetmeats.

My great-grandmother shows in her book that I may boast of kinship with the Siddons family. Elizabeth Grant's brother 'William' (Great-Great-Uncle William, I suppose)—whose sole claim to distinction when young seems to have been a short but pleasant sojourn in the Debtors' Prison of Edinburgh—eventually married Mrs. Siddons's granddaughter, Sarah, daughter of her eldest son, Henry, who married the actress Harriet Murray. My great-grandmother refers to Mrs. Henry Siddons's handling of the situation as follows:

My sisters and I had a subject of anxiety in William's engagement to Sally Siddons . . . I feared my mother would give way to a violence of disapproval that would make all concerned very uncomfortable, and that would upset my father . . . Mrs. Siddons had written to my father detailing the progress of the attachment, which she would not sanction without his consent. She touched on William's faults of character, but believed them to have been redeemed by the way in which he supported adversity. William was keeping his terms at the Temple, Lord Glenelg having obtained permission for him to proceed as a barrister to Bengal. The last paragraph of Mrs. Siddons's letter did probably no harm; it stated that Sally's fortune would be at least ten thousand pounds.

Though Mrs. Henry Siddons may not have had the gifts of her mother-in-law, she had certainly adopted some of the great actress's well-known technique of the frontal attack. The daughter-in-law was a match for an impoverished Highland family, touching as she did (with perfect timing) on 'William's faults' and hinting at her daughter's dowry—all within a few polite sentences.

The Siddons family appear more than once in the book; Mrs. Siddons, senior, emerges as a remarkable woman with no mean eye to business. Uncle William, perhaps, did well for himself by hooking Sally and her £10,000 dowry earned by the sweat of the great Siddons brow, for she once returned to the stage for a short period of time solely to embellish the fortunes of her grandchildren.

•   •   •

Back once more in the Royal Opera House, I learned the geography of this great rabbit warren of a theatre which has persistently come into my life through the years. A vast organization was growing up there; disturbing, in its energy, a few angry inhabitants. One night a large rat—rudely shaken by the general onslaught on his favourite haunts—decided to disrupt the performance: he dramatically rushed across the gallery, leaping over outstretched feet in his conception of a rodent Grand National; dexterously a zealous fireman caught him, for nothing could daunt the zeal of the Covent Garden firemen on their night and day vigil of retrieving six years' neglect of the underground haunts of the Royal Opera House: darkened haunts that also hold the echo of the voices of Melba and Caruso, and unforgettable visions of Karsavina and Nyjinska. . . .

Along the lengthy corridor upstairs, behind the rows of padlocked wooden doors, there rest the huge wardrobes of clothes that bear the indelible stamp of my old friends the Brothers Comelli. Incredible now appear the richness, the wealth of detail and the elaborate trimmings in these clothes of an opulent past. How immaculate is the tailoring of the men's coats, and how perfect the finish of the finely-boned bodices of Edwardian divas! When daylight first lights up these carefully guarded treasures the perfume of moth balls is strong in its attack; yet it becomes immediately faint—to die with swift relief upon the air of the present.

I am in the wardrobe when the doors of *La Traviata* are unlocked; I seek out my own costume of nearly forty years ago: I finger the delicately made chiffon roses trailing on the wide satin skirt; as I finger them I hear the Brothers Comelli tell me again how to wear my gipsy headdress. Suddenly Monsieur Ambroisine is showing me my dance, and I feel myself dealing the fortune-telling cards—carefully laying them out on the boards of the Opera House stage, as I did on the night of my twenty-first birthday.

At the moment of this theatre's re-opening, one or two familiar faces are still there to greet me as I return to this place destined to be my final theatrical goal; Mr. Jackson, the stage-door keeper, a friend of mine since the summer of 1919, and Mr. Ballard the chief machinist, who could peer into the depths of the stage and tell you what every rolled-up cloth would prove to be—if he unrolled it. All the mysterious regulations of the L.C.C. were tucked away in his head: he was consumed with the sacred flame of safety first, for his artists, his bridges, his traps and his flying appliances. The 'No' that Mr. Ballard said in 1919 rang with the same finality in 1946.

I will show, for a minute, something of our post-war group of artists at Covent Garden. Certain artists had, by now, left us; others were prepared, in fact interested, to take on different work. Notable among the latter were Ursula Moreton and Peggy van Praagh: these two had their hands full unravelling the problems of the newly formed second Company at Sadler's Wells Theatre; Ailne Phillips was in charge of the Ballet School, with Arnold Haskell as the newly appointed Director. From Russia, Vera Prokhorova, with her years of training and her graduation in the Bolshoi Ballet School in Moscow, was to infuse new blood into the Company and to become known to us as Violetta Elvin. From Paris, within six months, there came Harijs Plucis—ex-dancer from the Riga Opera House. He accepted a lengthy contract as academic professor to the Company and School, and also worked as one of the *répétiteurs* for the principals. Beryl Grey had grown into a commanding Lilac Fairy for the opening night of our season; Moira Shearer was to be presented, almost directly, as the Sleeping Beauty. Another Sleeping Beauty was Pamela May and we had a gracious Queen Mother in Julia Farron; she wore her lovely Messel costume with dignity, this 'little Farron' of yesterday, who in the Islington days had gone on tour in her fourteenth year and was heard to remark on that occasion that she would 'at last dance to an orchestra' . . . Jean Bedells, the one-time Clara of *Casse-Noisette*, was now the Countess in the wood scene.

We soon had reason to watch with interest the human freight coming off the few ships that had now reached us from Australia, New Zealand and South Africa.

Nadia Nerina may have won the Commonwealth race by a hair's-breadth; I see her standing as one of the two demure nurses in the prologue on the opening night of *The Sleeping Beauty*; later she was a soloist with the newly formed Wells Company. In quick succession we welcome Elaine Fifield, Rowena Jackson, Marion Lane, Dorothea Zaymes, Patricia Miller, Henry Legerton, Gilbert Vernon, David Poole and Joan Grantham. I can remember auditioning Alfred Rodrigues; I can see John Cranko in every type of *corps de ballet* rôle; I can recall hastily sending to the School for 'the boy from New Zealand' to come down to the Garden at once, as we wanted to put

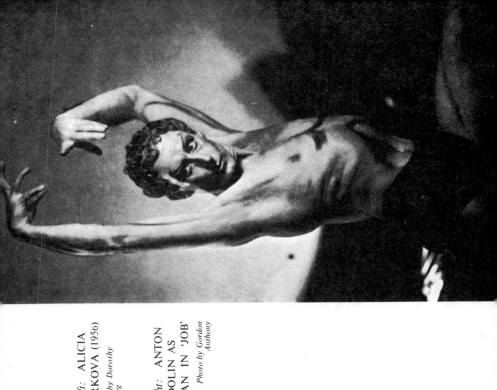

Left: ALICIA
MARKOVA (1956)

*Photo by Dorothy
Wilding*

Right: ANTON
DOLIN AS
SATAN IN 'JOB'

*Photo by Gordon
Anthony*

PEARL ARGYLE

SOPHIE
FEDOROVITCH

him on at a matinée in *The Three Ivans*. I added that he was so tough he would surely get through. Alexander Grant surely did, as he has hundreds of times since that afternoon.

There was something very moving in the efforts made by these young artists from this Commonwealth of ours; with all speed did they reach us after the cessation of the war. They put up with the roughest conditions on the boats, making journeys of several thousands of miles on chance, for they were not in a position to know, until they arrived in England and had an audition, whether or not they would qualify for the Sadler's Wells School and Ballet.

We had, however, avoided filling the gaps in the Companies with special talent from foreign countries; this was fortunate, as otherwise we would have lost the Commonwealth's avalanche of talent; most of these dancers joined the School for special periods of study, gradually working their way into permanent positions in either one or other of the two Companies.

It should be recorded that the Royal Academy of Dancing played a great part in this invasion of Commonwealth dancers; for many of them came over on Royal Academy Scholarship schemes.

Meanwhile our 'Bevin boys' (as we called the very young boys in the Company during the war) were compelled to leave us for their military training: in quick succession there went Brian Shaw, Michael Boulton, Ray Powell, Donald Britton, Peter Clegg and many others. These boys were already seasoned artists, in spite of the fact that they had been at the School in wartime.

Let us slip down to the School and watch some of the post-war enrolments. I find many of the entrants, in 1946, undersized children of poor physique, making nonsense of the reports that emphasised the high standard of nourishment.

Auditions are numerous and talent does not, at first, strike one as plentiful. It is now time, though, to make a note of those already in the School, who had enrolled during the last years of the war. There is the little girl that I had found in Manchester; she will do as a mouse for the Carabosse chariot (Annette Page was surely the smallest mouse that Carabosse ever caught). There is the young girl with the heart-shaped face—once Miss Scott Giles, according to the School list. In the Covent Garden Company she begins to assert herself as Rosemary Lindsay. The Coppélia doll of the New Theatre, Anne Heaton, joins the second Company. We decide to keep an eye on the 'Basque Boy' who answers to the name of Aldabalda-Trecku. His talent is as great as his capacity for being late for everything. His lengthy name on the board as an 'extra' causes consternation; for a long time he is to be known as Half-a-Pound-of-Treacle, the nearest the Company considers they can get towards digesting his surname. There is a talented boy from the Midlands who hates his extra book-learning at School, and tells Mr. Haskell so in no uncertain terms. Mr. Haskell stands firm; the extra schooling continues because it happens to be a part of the whole curriculum. David Butterworth capitulates, although never wholly convinced. Later, though, as David Blair, he sees the situation in better perspective.

What has happened to the small boy who used to live on the Bournemouth milk trains? Philip Chatfield (six feet in his socks) is now a fully-fledged member of the Company.

Now promoted to the second Company from the School is a thin, tall boy of great talent, by name Kenneth MacMillan. A little girl, who has been in America for some years, suddenly appears in our midst in the Junior School. She has Grecian features set above a long slender neck, her hair is wound about her ears as earphones—she is shy and retiring; she is described in school as 'a true classical type with a difficult back; a great talent for drawing, and will soon be ready to try for her School Certificate'. She obtained her School Certificate, continued to draw and to develop as a true classical type —and suddenly blossomed forth as Anya Linden.

One day in the foyer of Covent Garden I meet a young girl with her father. I have seen her dance elsewhere and noted that such poetry of motion and feeling was rare in one so young. . . . The personality is the same in private life; I hoped so much that one day she would be with us. The wish was fulfilled: for young Beriosova eventually joined the second Company—sharing the leading rôles with small, dark, fluid-moving, seventeen-year-old Elaine Fifield.

It was not very long before I began to realize that London had taken the establishment of a permanent ballet at the Royal Opera House very much to heart. Heavy economic restrictions still existed; yet the shortage of commodities made it all the easier for people to continue to spend money lavishly in the theatres. I noticed that our public consisted largely of those whom we had not been able to reach before the war. They were the many followers of the original Russian Companies who had never found their way out to Islington, and had had little opportunity of seeing us during the war years.

The prestige of the Company was mounting every week; yet we had what might be called a fairly thin line of defence. The continuation of National Service at this stage hit us very hard, spent as we were after the long war period. At this time there was yet no Opera Company formed; we performed, from 19th February until June, every night for about eighteen weeks. It was a great strain on a Company that was rather more than a third smaller in numbers than it is today: we also had to remount every ballet for the Opera House, a matter that again compelled us to exist on a very restricted repertoire.

•   •   •

With the spring of 1946, we were approaching the post-war productions of Frederick Ashton.

He had been given leave of absence from the R.A.F. just once during the war for a period of three months—when he mounted one important work for us. Fighting against time and the difficulties of creating anything on tour in wartime England, *The Quest* with music by William Walton, décor and costumes by John Piper, was not the success when produced (at the New Theatre) that it might have been in happier circumstances.

One of Ashton's first ventures for us at Covent Garden was on a particularly modest scale. He chose César Franck's *Symphonic Variations* using only six dancers and a very simple set by Sophie Fedorovitch. It proved, however, to be one of our major successes. Its abstract simplicity was completely satisfying; it spoke boldly from the huge stage, every movement sharply defining the ballet's lineal purity and the dancers filling space with the speed of meteors; here was a study in neo-classicism of the highest quality.

I have known Frederick Ashton from his first years as a student in the ballet world. I can remember him in the 'twenties, first as a pupil of Leonide Massine and later with Marie Rambert. Small, nervous and touchingly eager to please, is the picture that I recall of him. Like so many artists, he was more in love with his second best talent: for at one time he appeared to want to dance more than anything else in the world. When a member of Madame Rambert's Ballet Club, he would dance sometimes with me as an 'extra' in the early Old Vic Christmas Ballets—before Sadler's Wells was rebuilt. The Ballet Club gave its first performance at the Mercury Theatre about three months ahead of the opening of the Sadler's Wells Theatre.

Ashton joined the Vic-Wells Ballet the year that Markova left us in 1935. From that autumn, until the outbreak of war, we had the benefit of his first group of ballets. He was exceptionally prolific— always working with a great facility. He has never cared to wander far from his native ballet company, and when he has done so, he has always appeared to be profoundly miserable until he has returned home again.

Ashton has an intensely ephemeral attitude towards his ballets—I doubt if he has any notes of reference on any of them . . . he would prefer to re-compose rather than endeavour to remember.

He always says that his idea of happiness is to be in the *corps de ballet*. Some years ago I was standing next to him during a rehearsal of Purcell's *Faerie Queen* at the Royal Opera House. He was directing the choreography: an unconsciously humorous (to balletic minds anyway) rendering of a song was in progress, and although the *corps de ballet* were in a group on the stage, their faces were turned away from the auditorium. Suddenly a faint shaking was discernible —a ripple that increased in vibration as it noticeably passed through the bodies of the dancers. 'Look,' said Fred, 'they are having such a wonderful giggle—Oh, I wish I was still in the *corps* and able to giggle like that . . .'

Ashton's giggling days were spent in the Ida Rubinstein Company in the last years of the 'twenties. He and William Chappell were humble members of the Company. I can imagine them: two small English boys—inexperienced, half-trained and underpaid. He has told me of the economic embarrassment that was caused when the two of them had a quarrel, and might not be on speaking terms for some days: finances demanded the sharing of the tooth paste, the cake of soap and the hair oil; silence made all requests for such mundane possessions a matter of acute, though momentary, loss of dignity. . . .

In his early days Ashton might be lethargic about his choreography, but there was never as much as a hint of lethargy about his dancing. When young, his weakness lay in a difficulty in keeping time with the music—and the clock. Eagerness and intense nervous energy (his natural reaction to movement) made him deaf to sound; one would hold on to him grimly and at the same time experience something of the trouble encountered by anyone involved in the capture of a wild Dartmoor pony.

When I was at Covent Garden Opera House for the International Season of Opera in 1928, the management were requiring young male dancers for some special operas and I gave them the names of five. Ashton was one of the group, and went to see Colonel Blois (the Director) as spokesman for them all. He asked £5—and the Colonel offered £3. Full of fears, Ashton stood his ground—and won. I was greeted a week later by a young man who registered something between elation and panic; for he had just received his pay packet and it was clear that there had been a little misunderstanding: where Ashton had been discussing an acceptable weekly fee, the

Colonel had been reckoning in terms of a single performance. The boys' heavy pay packets left them pale, composed and discreetly silent; no doubt the Colonel considered that if there were only five male dancers in the country a little tough bargaining was to be expected: he therefore decided to meet the unseemly demand with an outward show of philosophical grace.

Ashton's love of the *corps de ballet* brings back another picture: one day that summer, overcome with mirth, he came towards me in a dimly lit scene in the opera *Armide*. He resembled a banshee conjured up by James Stephens—straight from the pages of *The Crock of Gold*. He was carrying innumerable woollen serpents that he had been told to manipulate—writhing choreographically at the same time behind gauzes. To save unnecessary hard work, Monsieur Ambroisine (the Belgian ballet master) was not above encouraging his dancers to improvise; Ashton and his little gang took every advantage of the old gentleman's failing: fortunately, the improvising, on this particular occasion, was dimmed by the sombre lighting and the thick gauzes. Perhaps I enjoyed it more than anyone—with my uninhibited view from the wings.

I like to think that it was destiny that made Frederick Ashton cross my path. As a boy he came all the way from South America to be a boarder at Dover College; during his schooldays I was still a frequent visitor to my grandmother's house in Walmer—seven miles away. Later in London (before we had actually met) his mother took a flat in Earl's Court Square: the Ashton family thus lived in a house only a few doors away from my own London home.

Few artists would have been capable of reaching Ashton's position of eminence, starting, as he did, when already settled in an office in the City. Few, of this generation, will leave such a definite mark on our balletic history. The potential historical significance of his contribution is immense, for he is a great classicist; it is through him that the style of the English Classical ballet derives its own individuality. Others may have produced ballets of a more national style in their choreography schemes and conceptions: yet it is the choreography of Ashton that has developed and enriched the main stream of the English style, expressing with sympathy and brilliant understanding the qualities of the English ballerina. He is, on the whole, less successful with the male dancer; the same, however, is known to be true of the great Petipa.

Ashton lost five important years of creative work when he was called up in the war. His work previously had been executed when the English Ballet was experimenting in all directions, and sometimes the process for a choreographer proved to be both tedious and painful. Yet the spirit behind all pioneer work is exceptionally virile; Ashton had the chance, as the most talented of us all in those early days, to fill a void: he was to create one much-needed ballet after another.

Twenty-five years ago choreographic mishaps were not so far-reaching in their effect as they are today; money was certainly short, yet productions could be very inexpensively mounted; furthermore new ballets were absolutely necessary, as no large repertoire of English ballets had yet been established. Now twenty-five years of work exist to form a background and tradition.

Today the young choreographer may have the backing of a subsidized institution, combined with fully-trained professional dancers in satisfying numbers; yet his opportunities need to be more carefully spaced out: this means that rapid progress, which is the result of trial and error, is not as easy for our young choreographers today as it was twenty-five years ago. On the other hand opportunity comes to the present-day choreographer many years in advance of our opportunities of yesterday. Ashton was thirty years of age before he produced *Les Rendezvous* for Sadler's Wells, and I was thirty-three before I produced *Job* for the Camargo Society, and, as already stated, I had to produce this work mainly on guest dancers for two isolated performances. A young choreographer of today would consider that very rough treatment: sometimes, though, I wonder if they get as much excitement as we did out of our efforts, surrounded, as we were, with every form of hazard.

•   •   •

The Sadler's Wells Ballet was to see, between 1947 and 1949, more travelling in Europe, and an ever widening field of international recognition. As I write it is nearly ten years since this period of its history: the pictures run one into the other and become more telling in swift panorama than if every detail is viewed in strictly tabulated order.

It was right that one of our first duties should be to return to Holland, where, again under the direction of the Beeks, we were to complete the tour that had proved to be so ill-timed at an earlier date. In The Hague I visited the café where a bullet that might have found a home in one of our heads once lodged . . . I met the proprietor; he had kept the bullet as a memento of his former loss of plate-glass.

There is the memory of our 1946 visit to Vienna, with the city under the first threat of the coming winter. This city was ruthlessly divided into three parts, with its principal hotels allotted respectively to the military requirements of the British, American and Russian armies. We were billeted in the British Hotel, the most charming and most characteristic of pre-1914 Vienna—the famous Hotel Sacher. Facing the hotel there remained only the walls of the great Vienna Opera House. In spite of the populace's want of food and everyday necessities, all Vienna gave weekly sums of money towards the resurrection of the Opera House, and all Vienna gave freely of some part of its scant free time (from the daily struggle of earning a livelihood) towards the clearing of the rubble. One received the impression that, through the re-establishment of their Opera House, the Viennese themselves would rise again.

We appeared in one of the smaller Opera Houses. The public was almost entirely Viennese; only a very small allotment of seats was given to the occupying forces. What a wonderful public they proved to be!

The Viennese Opera Company was also to be seen at this smaller Opera House—a veritable Phoenix rising from the ashes. I can recall my reactions to their productions: it seemed to me that I had encountered, for the first time, the true essence of opera production.

I was deeply impressed by a technique that showed a simplicity of
approach, economy and dignity of movement founded on a tradition of true operatic gesture; it placed opera production in a world of
its own. It was derived, of course, from the main technique of theatre
movement in general, yet one was made aware that it had developed
a form that was solely concerned with its own medium—solving
that problem of movement and gesture in relation to the singer. In
its perfected technique (as I saw it in Vienna) the singer's art of
gesture is as far removed from that of the actor, as the gesture of the
dancer is from either: one was made aware that there was a source
for all these singers to turn to and absorb—something hidden in the
operatic history of their theatre.

Other parts of Eastern Europe entered our world the same year.
Prague, Warsaw, Poznan, are the cities prominent in memory. In
Prague we found awaiting us Sasha Markov, the ballet master from
the Prague Opera House, who had been in England during the war
and who had, at that time, produced *The Bartered Bride* for the
Sadler's Wells Opera Company. In Warsaw Leon Woijikowski was
standing on the platform as the train drew in to the station. Leon
had been in Poland for the whole of the war; but his name was
legendary to most of our young post-war company. The sight of him
standing there called forth a shout from me: quickly the news spread
along the corridor who this man was that I engaged in such a lengthy
conversation—the great Woijikowski of the Diaghilev Ballet.

Life in Warsaw was grim: the little Opera House that we danced
in had already been rebuilt once, and the main big one had disappeared under the fierce bombardments that the city had been subjected to so often. Warsaw was veritably in ruins . . . a city that now
showed a struggle for mere existence; it seemed impossible that
human beings in their thousands could continue to live there, yet
they did, sleeping seven and eight to one unlit and unheated room.
Most of the younger men and women had two jobs: thus they
worked a sixteen-hour day so as to meet the price of food and cloth-

ing. I saw the notorious Jewish ghetto that had been sealed off and bombarded unceasingly for forty-eight hours—until all was finished. One could stand on a monument of bricks, thirty feet high, and look over the enormous area; it consisted of a desert of similar mounds covering some two square miles. I have never experienced such an unearthly silence—uncanny, terrible; it settled on one like the silent reproach of thousands of beings, a reproach that had become a part of space itself.

The Poles were wonderful to us; and one of the most exciting and gratifying performances was the one that we gave at three-thirty in the afternoon. The audience consisted of men and women between the ages of twenty and thirty; they came to the theatre between their work shifts. What an audience they made! There were also late evening concerts for these people: the theatre was a part of the life of the populace—it was unthinkable to go without it.

Lovely Prague was, of course, more prosperous—with all its theatres open and its beautiful city intact. High up in the old town, commanding one of the finest views of Prague from its gardens, there stands the British Embassy, surely the most perfect of all our Embassies. Sir Philip Nichols was our Ambassador there. A delightful reception was held in our honour one warm early autumn evening after the ballet performance, which had been attended by the diplomatic corps and many Czechs. I can hear a young South African dancer exclaim: 'I never thought that by coming to England I would finish up at the British Embassy in Prague . . . I shall never forget tonight.'

We were fortunate in these travels; for all too soon after our return all such places were cut off from Western Europe. The inevitable, of course, was already written on many faces that we met daily. It was in Warsaw that a Polish woman said to me swiftly and softly: 'It is good that you come, because when we applaud you we feel that we speak to you not only as artists but as England . . .'

I returned from Poland via Berlin and the Company worked its way back via Sweden and Norway. Interest in the ballet was very marked in Scandinavia: at the Royal Theatre in Oslo one thousand people were outside the theatre very early in the morning awaiting the opening of the box-office for the first time.

Europe was reaching out in other directions towards the English ballet. I was receiving continuous requests to assist in either the establishment or re-establishment of National Schools of Ballet. Two of these invitations were of the greatest interest, and these were the ones which it was decided that I should seriously consider.

•   •   •

At the invitation of the Turkish Government and with the assistance of the British Council, I set off in the May of 1947 to visit Istanbul, to lay the foundations of a National School of Ballet for the Turks.

People regarded my venture as an Arabian Night's Tale; in fact nobody took the matter very seriously but myself, and I imagine the Turks . . . or at least someone in Turkey who had once thought about it, and who had passed the idea on to someone, who no doubt wished that the first one had not thought about it at all.

I flew to Istanbul, to be greeted at the airport by Dr. Phillips (British Council) and three Turks standing in a row; the middle one was rather self-consciously clutching a huge bunch of red roses. These three gentlemen were delegates from the Ministry of Fine Arts, so we were off to a dignified start.

Dr. Phillips told me that, when the plane arrived, I was preceded down the gangway by a stout lady in an enormous cartwheel hat. The three Turks remained impassive; yet a vague feeling of oriental apprehension could be sensed at the sight of this lady in full sail. 'Is that,' asks one Turk very slowly, with a markedly impersonal

tone of voice, 'is that Madame de Valois?' 'Good gracious, no!' says
Dr. Phillips boldly, having never set eyes on me in his life. The Turk
did not register anything, but he was heard to murmur firmly and
fervently 'Thanks be to Allah'.

I think that Turkey gives a wonderful introduction to its ancient
capital if you reach Istanbul by car from the airfield. Lovely is the
city's outline for those who first see it against the sky from the sea;
but this other way you are greeted by its magnificent crumbling city
wall where the gipsies have encamped themselves with their houses
which are a part of the old wall itself.

Istanbul in the spring! I have seen it thus quite often and yet it
gets me afresh each time by the heart strings: there is its tumbling
luscious wistaria falling in unruly cascades after a mighty climb up
some high wall, or the sides of a house; then the old wooden houses,
wonderful examples of seventeenth-century work—gratefully and
graciously do they seem to stretch out their elegant timbered façades
towards the warm sun rays. Many of these ancient homes of the
pashas, face, in all their beauty, on to the Bosphorus, with the waters
still lapping gently against the ledges of their long, elegant windows.
There are the little ferry boats in their interminable trips up and down
the Bosphorus. You sit on board and wait for the boat to pick up
the Asiatic peasant, who carries anything from flowers to an iron
bedstead on his back, and, on occasions, appears to remove the
entire belongings of his household on the combined backs of his
family.

I awoke, that first morning in Istanbul's Park Hotel, to a medley
of street noises that other visits have since helped to analyse: the cry
of the water carrier, the fish carrier and the goatherd—all wending
their way up through the old wooden town which reaches down to
the busy Bosphorus, where the sound of sea commerce asserts itself
above the hurly-burly of that special noise which is Istanbul. Then
at dawn and at sunset the call from the minaret, a sound that goes
back through the centuries, remote from other sounds bred by the
increasing demands of man's daily requirements.

I was to begin, on that spring day, a task that I had allotted myself three weeks to accomplish. I had in my possession a long piece of parchment, with the stamp on it of the Turkish Government: this was the contract that held me to my pledge of laying down the principles of this school. Dr. Phillips knew the East well, spoke Turkish, and was prepared to be immensely helpful . . . but he begged me to curb my enthusiasm and develop an understanding of procrastination as a highly skilled game that I would no doubt encounter played with a consummate ease.

One of my first tasks was to visit the head of the Istanbul Fine Arts Academy; this was to be followed by an interview with some vague ministerial set-up. Once through these two ordeals, I would attend a cocktail party given to me by the British Council, where I would meet artists, musicians, writers, the press and plenty of officials in whose offices I would also have to sit and listen to the interminable interpreting. I would next be let loose on the country, to visit primary schools and inspect the children. I would then go to Ankara and start everything all over again, but the schools this time would be secondary and lycée. Finally I would return to Istanbul and write out a long report; the report would be translated into Turkish at the British Council, and would then be sent to those offices and ministries that I had visited during my three weeks stay in the country.

I was fortunate with the head of the Academy of Fine Arts: when he grasped, or perhaps just remembered, why I was there—he was charming, enthusiastic and most helpful. I was also grateful to find that he was as determined that I should see something of the treasures of his country, as I was that his country should have this requested National School of Ballet. We were both aware of the distance that I had come and that time must be well spent.

The discussions that followed with other officials were always to the accompaniment of endless cups of Turkish coffee: when the silent Asiatic servant entered carrying the brass tray with its tiny cups, I would breathe a sigh of deep relief and consume my cupful in its stickiest state of sweetness—so as to fortify myself for the task of assisting Dr. Phillips to bring back the Turks from that lethargic timelessness of Turkey and the consumption of coffee, to the endless matters concerning my mission. Turks in a circle tend to think in a circle, geared to a remarkably low speed; it is not the slightest use to entertain any hope of a sudden acceleration.

Eventually, however, some progress was made. I had stood for my four hours at the cocktail party; I had talked to the press—divided as the press always is on such occasions into interest, scepticism, economic disapproval and even political intrigue on a very minor scale. I had talked to the artists and the innumerable directors of the arts and crafts in general.

Then at last I was on my way to see my first Turkish primary school, at Yesilkoy—the little village on the sea of Marmora so near the main airport station. This state primary school, for boarders, was to be for some two or three years the headquarters of the Ballet School. It is right on the sea, situated on a piece of rising ground, a bare-looking, pleasant Turkish house. Living conditions for the children were gloriously simplified—and, in many ways, rather to be envied by anyone familiar with the endless complications of such institutions in England. Large, very high, bare rooms hold dozens of small children; their dormitory conditions would have kept our County Councils in a state of frenzied bureaucracy for months. The children's sleeping bunks were two-tiered and covered the entire room; the uncurtained windows were very large and open to the sea breezes. Furniture seemed non-existent, and life appeared to solve the problem of the cubic foot by ignoring its existence.

The children, in their primary school uniforms of black and white, looked healthy enough, clean enough and full of life. The little boys, with their well-shaped shaven heads, varied in feature and colour from sandy-haired European types to Asiatics with features belonging to Anatolia and the Black Sea coast. The girls were not so attractive; but an occasional startling sultry beauty could be discovered, with roving expressive eyes—black sloes dancing to some purpose already in the otherwise unawakened little face.

My inspection of these children started; it also continued, for some days, in other primary schools near Istanbul. The idea was that any children considered suitable would be removed to Yesilkoy, and housed there in a special group to be known as the Ballet School section. Many of the daily primaries that I visited were not of the high standard of the boarding one at Yesilkoy. The children often appeared to come from very poor homes; they were very shy, and the removal of their frequently threadbare footwear nearly reduced them to tears; much of the consternation was caused by the fact that they knew that their feet were not always clean, and they would curl their toes up as they stood there, until they almost disappeared. I would touch their insteps; once they realized that I was indifferent to their dust-ingrained feet, the toes would slowly relax and the face sometimes break into a great broad smile.

I crossed by night train to Ankara and the inspection continued. Towards the end of my work in Ankara I was brought by car to a college for adults set in the hills about fifty miles outside the city. Here higher education and agricultural courses were given to hundreds of young men and women from the surrounding villages; at the completion of their studies they had to return to their own small towns or villages, to put their acquired knowledge into practice.

When we arrived a great horn was blown and the students came in from the fields and classrooms and foregathered in a big hall. The young men and women (for it was a co-educational college) were dressed in identical uniforms—a form of very light slate coloured pyjama suit made of what appeared to be a coarse mixture of cotton and linen. I then spent an enthralling two hours. The students divided themselves into many groups, and each group was representative of some particular part of Anatolia. To the accompaniment of a variety of different musical instruments—each instrument associated with one particular district—a group would execute its district's national dances. These dances were mostly for men, and many of them very skilful and exciting to watch. At the end they formed a huge circle; they then started a simple ring-dance accompanied by a gay chant, which was directed, with many smiles, towards me. I was informed that it was an old native song inviting me to dance with them—I learnt the dance moving round with them in the circle.

The whole visit, set as it was in a valley midst those ever-changing Anatolian hills of rich blue and mauve tints, was an experience that one day I hope to repeat.

After a lengthy conversation with the Minister of Education and the Fine Arts, I returned to Istanbul to draw up the memorandum.

By the following autumn of 1948 the school was opened in Yesilkoy under the direction of two English teachers; Joy Newton, who had been the Sadler's Wells Ballet mistress for eight years (and before that one of the six original dancers of 1931) volunteered to go out as director of the school taking with her an assistant, Audrey Knight, a young teacher trained by the Royal Academy of Dancing. They did the heavy pioneer work, and Miss Newton stayed until the school was officially recognized by Turkish law—four years later. The children then moved to the Ankara Conservatoire where they are now housed in that very good building, with the students of music and drama.

The school is still under English direction; it now employs four English teachers who are also responsible for the opera ballets in Ankara's attractive Opera House. The present director is Travis Kemp—one-time member of the Sadler's Wells Ballet—together with Molly Lake, his wife (an ex-member of Pavlova's company). They are in charge of the Conservatoire School, and the young artists pass from there to the opera ballet. The students graduate after nine years of study at the Conservatoire, where they also receive their general education.

We have found Turkish children responsive to the Western musical idiom, and, as in all cases of supply where there is a sudden demand, the right type of physique is coming well to the fore. The boys are naturally athletic; there should be, one day, a good supply of male dancers. It has been harder work with the girls; the country, though, has a great deal of mixed racial blood; patience and careful selection is now bringing forth something that will reward the Turkish Government one day for their efforts.

DAME MARGOT
FONTEYN, D.B.E.

FREDERICK
ASHTON, C.B.E.

OLIVER MESSEL
Photo by Tony Armstrong Jon

FIRST PERFORMANCE OF 'THE SLEEPING BEAUTY',
FEBRUARY 19, 1946, AT THE ROYAL OPERA HOUSE

Kemsley Picture Service

It is an interesting venture, and it is the first National School of Ballet in a foreign country that England has established.

I have always found the Turks good company and they have a great sense of humour. Their attitude towards time, however, has a special subtlety of its own, as is best explained by the following story.

A young Turk, studying at Harvard, made himself known to me one night in New York at the Metropolitan Opera House, when the Ballet was there on its second visit. During our conversation he informed me that he was just about to return to Turkey. When I asked him if he would fly back, he explained that he would not do so and then told me something of his plans. He would go by boat to England, and then by boat to France. He would travel by train to Marseilles and from there take a slow boat to Genoa . . . and from Genoa he would take a small boat that would stop at many places before it reached Istanbul . . . his journey was to take eight weeks. 'You see,' he added, 'I would not fly—it is such a waste of time. . . .' Would that we were all as wise.

To illustrate their humour I would tell of the dignitary from the Ministry of Fine Arts who had once taken a voyage to America in connection with his work. On board the ship some American women (from the Middle West) asked him if it was true that he was a Turk. When he said that this was so, they inquired as to the exact number of his wives. 'Seven,' he promptly informed them, 'one for each day in the week.' The ladies were overcome by the thought of the possible expense involved, so he explained that he expected his wives to keep him. 'You see,' he explained to me, with a face creased with good humour, 'it was so very necessary for me to feed their imagination.'

My next adventure was concerned with a visit to Yugoslavia. The request came from the Yugoslav National Theatres and, on our side, was sponsored by the British Council.

I was to visit the State Ballet Schools of Ljubljana, Zagreb, and

14

Belgrade. The visit was to be quite informal and was in the nature of a friendly survey of the existing state of the ballet, with the added request to report on any necessary innovations. I was to be given every opportunity to meet the teachers, choreographers and dancers, as well as the official personalities.

In 1950 travelling to Yugoslavia via Germany was still on a war-time basis. I had to fly to Frankfurt and there to spend one night in a city devastated by the war and still under military control. There was no British Council representative in the town, therefore billeting arrangements were made from the London headquarters. I arrived clutching a green ticket; this ticket confirmed that somewhere in the town there was a bedroom at my disposal for the night. Filled with an ever mounting scepticism, and feeling very isolated, I decided that before embarking on some sort of vehicle in search of the green card address, I would inquire about my plane to Yugoslavia on the following morning. It was just as well that I took the precaution, for although I had the necessary ticket, my name, on inquiry, did not appear on the passenger list. It took me half an hour to get it on; I then got into a German taxi which was to carry me to my night's lodgings.

Scepticism on that late winter Sunday afternoon soon turned to despondency: we went on and on, out into the suburbs amid scenes of bombed-out desolation that made, in comparison, the scarred parts of the City of London look like pleasantly constructed open spaces. The taxi eventually drew up in front of a seven-story mansion that could have been labelled 'A Present from South Kensington'. The adjoining house had been neatly shaved off by some high explosive. The house was desolate, and it had a façade of boarded-up windows that made it appear to be haphazardly bandaged and splintered.

From my vantage point on the pavement I could not discern any signs of life, nor did my green slip appear to have any further clue to offer me. Looking up I suddenly saw a German youth—suitably attired for an appearance in *White Horse Inn*—leaning out of a top window. 'Hi!' I shrieked, 'do you speak English?' 'I guess!' came back in a fair enough American accent. 'Well,' I continued, 'will you come down here?' Being a German he complied. He was very nice, heard my tale of woe, looked at my green slip, and then told me that he would take me to Frau Somebody's flat. The door of the flat was opened by a little woman who stood in a minute hall with five rooms built off it in a neat semi-circular effect. The words 'British Council' seemed to clarify everything for her. I was shown into one of the tiny rooms built off the hall. It was scrupulously clean and contained just a bed, a table and a curious stove in one corner that reminded me, in shape, of the stoves that I used to see in Edwardian dolls' houses. This stove was attached to a flue that vaguely disappeared into the wall. The little room was very cold; my Frau bustled in with some sticks and stuffed them into one mysterious compartment of the little stove and a crackling small fire was the result. She opened many small doors in the contraption, smiling and shaking her head as to their uselessness; she brightly mimed the descent of bombs as the reason for all this ineffectuality. I felt that all the bombs had been my personal doing, and longed to change the conversation that we were carrying on in a strange dumb-crambo. I was eventually left, after receiving further mimetic gestures that appeared to hold the promise of a meal.

I inspected my tiny bed; it had clean cotton sheets and pillow cases, the latter were edged with hideous crochet frills; I visualized a long grim evening ahead of me, yet for one hour (in which I was given a good supper) I had no idea as to the extent of its trials.

Suddenly there was much whispering behind my door and at last a timid tap: opened, the scene revealed a thin man and a fat woman, another man and my smiling frau. I realized that the contents of the Lilliputian flat had collected *en masse* in the hall. One of the men stepped forward; gravely he informed me that he spoke a little English and that they wished me to spend the evening with them in one of the rooms—he then bowed solemnly to the thin man and the fat woman. I said that I was very touched and thanked them. We trooped into the married couple's small bedroom; it contained the largest double bed in the world, a very large cupboard, a round table and four upright chairs. From the top of the cupboard someone brought down Bohemian hock glasses; down to the cellar went the English-speaking one, to return with a bottle of hock.

I was then informed that they would teach me the German word for everything in the room whilst we sipped the wine. The idea appeared to be full of humour; so I permitted my anyway shaky pronunciation to run riot, realizing the hilarity that my unresponsive ear appeared to be giving everyone. The evening wore on and the wine wore off, and the number of objects in the room that I could mispronounce was also eventually exhausted. My English-speaking friend suggested the wireless. They turned on to Eastern Germany and I listened to anti-British abuse from a woman who appeared to be English. She only stopped to draw breath, and even then her theme was carried on by an Englishman. Bland, smiling faces sur-rounded me—none more bland and smiling than the one who spoke English. He thought, no doubt, that I must still be badly in need of entertainment—what could be better than some in my own lan-guage? The woman speaker by now had returned refuelled with new flights of fantasy; she announced that the English were all work-ing in fearful conditions, the workers in slave labour camps run by the capitalists . . . with this statement even the wireless gave up the ghost—with a series of protesting crackles.

I sensed now that everyone had realized that the question of suitable entertainment was presenting fresh difficulties. My English speaker, however, was undaunted; he leapt to his feet and went to collect a huge scrapbook. 'Me,' he said, with a perfect orgy of bland smiles, 'come from Trieste.' Something that felt like butterflies in my stomach, and something else, resembling a too tight permanent hair wave, crept on me. The book was opened. I was shown newspaper cuttings, horror pictures of piled up dead bodies. I looked at my host, he still smiled, and with a bright nonchalance kept saying: 'Dead German men, all dead, bombs, English bombs . . .' To this day I shall never know if this gesture was made to show me the thorough work of British bombs, or if he was courting pity, or merely displaying his philosophical capacity to accept defeat: I looked and felt like a trapped goat, and somehow got the conversation back to the necessity of an early night's rest.

The next morning they all turned out to see me off, at the hour of 5.30 a.m. I presented my little Frau with six new lace-edged handkerchiefs: she wept, as if she was parting from an old friend.

My Yugoslav plane landed me at a very small aerodrome; I was greeted by three officials who gave me the impression that, unlike my three Turks, they would have been perfectly satisfied if I had resembled the large lady in the cartwheel hat.

My visit was to last three weeks. I was soon to discover that life was very hard and that the artists wanted many things—such as good ballet shoes and a higher ration of basic foodstuffs. The three State Schools were well organized and their senior professors mainly ex-members of the pre-revolution Imperial Ballets of Russia. I met with great friendliness and enthusiasm from the staff; I was struck with their devotion to their pupils, and the longing, among the younger teachers, to discuss the pedagogy of the dance elsewhere today. It was good sound old Russian School, ripe, however, for certain innovations. In the school there was a great deal of talent, despite the intense disruption caused through the war. The general standard and size of the school rose in each town, ending in Belgrade which possessed by far the most satisfactory National Ballet in the country.

For the first half of my visit (Ljubljana and Zagreb) I was attended from morn to night by an official female interpreter. She displayed a naïve zeal for her chosen political views. She belonged to the University group; her father had been a professor of science, who, she informed me brightly, had taught her the futility of religion. She was kind, earnest and muddled. Her eyes would fill with tears and her nose redden painfully at the prospect of losing a fragment of a point in an argument. At first, aware that she was a nice person fundamentally, I let her ramble and have it all her own way; but the constant companionship, and the accumulated senseless drippings of communism at last lashed up my logic in defence of democracy: I found myself gently calling her bluff. I asked her about rations and the price of foodstuffs. 'First,' she said, 'we buy our rations at the controlled prices, and then we buy extra rations—that is very expensive.' 'So,' I said, 'if you have plenty of money you get as many rations as you want—we are not allowed to do that. . . .' The eyes would fill with tears, the nose redden and the conversation would change. Peasants shocked her, they were so lazy; they never worked hard in the winter and they did not want to go into the lovely new factories. They wanted to stay on the land even in the winter, and to live in their peasant huts, where the only light that they had in the evening came from candles. They liked sitting in their candlelit huts. I said that we knew about the pastimes of the peasants—because the whole world had seen their lovely embroidery, done, I imagined, by candlelight, during the long winter evenings sitting in their peasant homes. I added that among the most beautiful sights that I had seen were the girls in the villages of Yugoslavia on a Sunday—swinging down the streets like peacocks in their many petticoats and their bright home-made traditional peasant costumes; I said that they matched the wild colourful countryside with its swift-flowing streams and rivers, and that I could not see what the factories had got to do with it . . . I then had to stop, because of a pathetic, frustrated pair of watering eyes and a mind filled with text book answers to the use and misuse of life's proffered diversions. Here was a human being whose mind had been subjected to imprisonment and, at an early age, must have suffered the erection of a form of impregnable wall. Time had hardened the plaster, which was once, perhaps, soft and pliable; there was no possible means now of dislodging any part of the wall so as to let in any vision of the outside landscape. Yet underneath it all she was just an earnest schoolmarm, serving the cause with hysterical fanaticism—a woman whom disillusionment might mentally derange.

Yugoslavia and communism seemed strange companions. Such a naturally friendly, gay and virile people; I loved my time spent with the young artists, and they were not in any way prevented from getting to know me. I was always allowed a question period with the dancers, and, although the teaching staff were present, the dancers always appeared to be perfectly at ease; they asked me anything that they wanted to know about Sadler's Wells and our dancers' lives— and they knew many of our leading dancers by name.

I spent Easter in Zagreb; an Easter to be remembered for its packed churches—packed particularly with the grey-clad army of young soldiers.

In Ljubljana and Zagreb I stayed, with my interpreter, at official hotels reserved by the government for visitors. In Belgrade I was the guest of Sir Charles and Lady Peake at the British Embassy. They made my visit a very happy one, and their interest and knowledge of the Belgrade Ballet was very helpful; the Embassy always had four tickets allotted to them for every performance. In Belgrade I had, as interpreter, a charming and lovely young girl (since married to an American) who was, at that time, secretary to the Ballet School.

I was, during the last few days of my Belgrade visit, officially presented by the Ministry of Fine Arts with a beautifully embroid- ered full-length velvet coat; covered with the fine gold embroidery that is said to take five years to execute. I thought of candlelight, my indignant friend, and the factories churning out cheap, modern articles. . . . The technical staff, on their own, gave me an attractive leather winter jacket, thickly lined with lambswool and covered with peasant embroidery.

On my last day in Belgrade I had an interview with an important minister: he wished to hear my views in general on the National Ballet companies. I presented myself at the Ministry and was ushered through a series of double doors, all heavily guarded. When I eventu- ally reached the office I found the minister sitting at a large desk under a life-sized portrait of Marshal Tito; the likeness between the two was so startling that I thought, for one moment, that fate had played me an odd trick. I praised the devoted and unselfish work of the teaching staffs and spoke of our interesting conferences, where many technical points had been discussed in an atmosphere of perfect harmony. I then begged him to look to the condition of the dancers' footwear, and informed him that the ballet shoes were so roughly made that they were seriously impeding the progress of the dancers. 'Madam,' he informed me brusquely, 'we make excellent turbines—therefore we must be able to make excellent ballet shoes.' In his cold steel-grey eyes I could see the blunt reckoning at work . . . a small object that was not perfect: there was some lack of organization, a routine machine matter at fault that required a little firm bureaucratic handling. Craftsmanship did not enter into it; it might well be that someone was lazy—like the peasants.

I left Belgrade for Greece—where I had been asked by the British Council to give two lectures. It was a wonderful journey by train, straight through to Athens, and from there I went on to see how things were progressing in Turkey.

•   •   •

The wheel turns and certain highlights reassert themselves. Once again in London there is a State visit by the French President, and an evening at the Royal Opera House is one of the official functions.

The Opera House is receiving its second high polish in a short period of time. . . . On the morning of the Gala all was chaos—for Oliver Messel's decorations were behind schedule. I pass along one of the passages of the Opera House: on the floor are a bevy of London's characteristic cleaners. These women, on all fours, in their sombre clothes, carpet slippers and canvas aprons resemble miniature jeeps. As I pass them the following comment is ejaculated during the wringing out of the mop: 'Come on with it, it's up to us to get open t'night; if we don't open—it's a International Crisis—that's what it is.' The jeeps in general guffaw, renew the attack, and break off suddenly for the inevitable brew of nigger-brown tea. I pass on my way with a sudden feeling of sentiment: I know that it is not beyond them

CONSTANT LAMBERT

TWO STUDIES OF
ROBERT HELPMANN

*Photo on right by
Gordon Anthony*

PAMELA MAY WITH CAROLINE

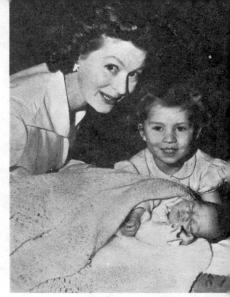

Central Press Photos Ltd

MOIRA SHEARER WITH AILSA
MARGARET AND RACHEL KATHERINE

BERYL GREY WITH INGVAR

P. A. Renter Photos Ltd.

URSULA MORETON WITH DAVID

MARGOT FONTEYN'S WEDDING PARTY
Ashton, Fonteyn, the Author, Edwards, Gilbert, Somes

SADLER'S WELLS THEATRE BALLET 1951, ON BOARD 'THE EMPRESS OF CANADA
Group includes: The author, Peggy Van Praagh, Elaine Fifield, Patricia Miller,
David Blair, David Poole, Annette Page, Marion Lane, Donald Britton

to throw off the jeep posture and to be found, late that evening, in an upright position on the edge of the kerb outside—'a'cheering', as they would say.

Again after fifteen years 'The Islington Dancers', now part and parcel of the great Covent Garden Market, supply the entertainment, with the trumpet players opening the proceedings with their fanfare in front of the red and gold curtains, and the Yeomen of the Guard installed at the top of the main stairways. . . .

Some days later, I receive from Noel Coward a charming note stressing the pride of the English Theatre in their National Ballet. I am reminded of the picture of 'The Goldfish' of long ago—with the little boy in the foreground dressed as a jester, whom the Principal called Noel; a boy that I sighed about as I executed my exercises at the barre—because I was told how clever he was and how well he was getting on in the theatre world. . . .

Guest artists were now invited to appear with us—in particular those guest artists whom England so much wanted to see again.

There was one night when, in breathless expectation, the curtains parted on Massine, taut and concentrated against the familiar décor of Picasso's *Tricorne*. The house was swept back over the years—it was again the golden era of Diaghilev; a tumult of applause broke out suspending any sort of action either on the stage or in the orchestra pit. Danilova likewise received a rapturous reception in *Coppélia*; Markova and Dolin returned in *Giselle*.

There is a picture of André Derain, in homburg and overcoat, delicately applying his brush to a bouquet of flowers painted on his *Mademoiselle Angot* front cloth: there is Christine Bérard in the wardrobe, all bustle, charm and kindliness.

Much later there is Lubov Tchernichave and Serge Grigorieff taking a curtain call after the first night of *Firebird*, which they had so lovingly and perfectly reproduced for us in conjunction with Karsavina—who had personally taught her famous rôle to Fonteyn;

Tamara Karsavina, working with all that gracious sincerity and concentration which is the hallmark of her unique personality.

I must not forget our twenty-first birthday; fittingly celebrated at the Sadler's Wells Theatre.

Suddenly it was a night reminiscent of those pre-war days, with everyone back in their old rôles and everyone arriving from everywhere to rehearse. . . . There was a house that was suffocatingly full; full, though, only of friends from the past—those members of the audience who had followed our fortunes through the years and were determined to make a great night of the occasion. There is the touching memory, that evening, of Fonteyn once more as the Little Boy in *The Haunted Ballroom*. Everyone seemed to be back in *The Wedding Bouquet*, and the Orgy Scene from *The Rake's Progress* took us back to the opening night in 1935.

I left next day for Turkey again on one of my periodical visits: I carried with me the glow of the tempestuous rowdiness of the night before—one of those rare moments in life that nothing could ever obliterate.

•   •   •

Vivid is the recollection of the Royal Opera House on the Coronation night of Queen Elizabeth II . . . The broadcast of her 9 p.m. speech from the Opera House auditorium . . . and the immediate parting of the curtain on our Coronation ballet *Homage to the Queen* danced by the entire Company. In sharp contrast to that night at Sadler's Wells in 1936, where, at a ballet performance, King Edward VIII's abdication speech was broadcast from the stage at 10 p.m., to a silent, despondent public.

•   •   •

The Ballet Theatre of America proved to be our first guest ballet Company, bringing with it our first contact with the long-limbed, slim dancers of the States, their vitality, their slick technique, their strong rhythm, and their humour—expressed as sparsely in American movement as it is in American words. That was in the summer of· 1946. We were still to await our return call, though rumour had it that effort was bringing it closer every month.

Our Company and the School continued to grow in size; the repertoire fluctuated as all repertoires do; but there was a steady feeling of expansion, of the signs of a tree with a sturdy root: with Frederick Ashton's version of Prokofiev's *Cinderella*, we launched in 1949 our first three-act ballet by a native choreographer.

•　　•　　•

It is early autumn in 1949 and we find ourselves preparing for the invasion of America. The second visit of Sol Hurok, the great American impresario, was to prove more fruitful than his first: on the previous occasion we had turned down the offer to appear at the City Centre—on a stage that was a great deal too small for our productions.

My first meeting with Hurok had been round about 1946–47. I do not think that we made any great impression on each other. Sol was, understandably, cautious with all ballet directors and managements, and perhaps I was even more cautious with impresarios. I can remember having lunch with him at the Savoy; during lunch he informed me that Sadler's Wells had a queer sort of idealism about it—and then left his statement unqualified. Neither the tone of his voice nor his expression suggested that he had knocked up against anything in the way of a revelation. I did not attempt to pursue the subject; I could understand, in view of his Russian Ballet experiences, that he found the unity of our Company slightly eccentric, in fact it must have struck him as odd that no one seemed to want to go elsewhere to seek his fortune, unless everyone else concerned came along at the same time: even the management wanted to appear in America on its own terms and in its own time, and in a theatre of its own choice. Hurok, although deeply interested in the full-length classics, did request me to curtail some of *The Sleeping Beauty*—I suggested that we could leave it behind, or if he preferred, we need not open in New York with it—but, I added, there would be no changes made for its presentation in New York . . . so, in the end, it went intact.

Preparations for America were not without humour. Our war-time rationing was still in full force—good clothes were scarce, and there was, in the country, a feverish accent on export. The treasury wanted dollars, the manufacturers wanted trade, and the English Theatre hoped for increased theatrical prestige. All looked to the Ballet—meanwhile the Ballet was thinking yearningly of T-steaks.

Pandemonium broke loose: in vain I stepped up the rehearsal schedules in an effort to bring everyone up to the highest pitch of perfection. Every fashion house was determined to dress the Ballet, to photograph the Ballet when dressed, and to load them with every-thing that accented the coming trend of fashion in British wools and tweeds.

Gamely the girls boarded the plane clad in Scotch sweaters, woollen coats and dresses, smart macs and with even smarter tartan umbrellas. It threatened to be a dangerously warm October. Once the plane took off the stewards on board showed visual signs of uneasiness as a frantic strip-tease act appeared to have started up among these forty smartly-clad young women. Discipline prevailed though: with that British sense of fair play the descent to the American aerodrome was made with all those umbrellas, macs, felt hats, travelling coats, sweaters and tweeds (smelling of the moors) much in evidence.

We had six days to prepare ourselves for the Sunday night opening at the 'Met' on 7th October.

We were overwhelmed with kindness; everyone who has ever been to America knows to what lengths that kindness can go. They were so generous that they immediately bestowed on me something that, for the first time in my life, I heard called a 'virus'. I was really ill for four days—with a temperature that at one point reached 104° and then settled down to a fairly steady 102°. Everyone sent me long cardboard coffins; these coffins proved to contain flowers of the most exotic kind. There would emerge long-stemmed roses, so long-stemmed that it seemed impossible that they would remember, at the topmost peak of the journey, the fact that they had to emerge as rosebuds; strange flora in porcelain pots with 'instructions' as to means of giving them a few hours of protection against a possible outburst of vicious central heating. Even the Russians had caught this exotic malady: I was a little unhappy that my old friends of the cheap Paris hotels of Russian Ballet days thought it necessary to deluge me with expensively filled cardboard coffins before they rang me up on the telephone.

Our fateful opening night has arrived; we see the interior of the 'Met' illuminated, and the famous diamond horse-shoe circle filled to the brim of each box. The red and gold of the theatre is comforting, so is the backstage, with that musty-smelling atmosphere of a great, sprawling Opera House, that has absorbed the traditions of world-wide Grand Opera. It is the same atmosphere (of decaying gold leaf and red velvet) that hangs around Covent Garden.

There is a feeling of intense excitement in the House that mounts with the humid heat of the Indian summer night.

For once we feel that all the eyes of New York and London are upon us, and the telegrams from England have been legion. In the box next to me sits Sir Oliver Franks, our Ambassador in Washington, who has come up for the opening performance. On the other side is Mr. O'Dwyer—the Irish Mayor of New York; he has arranged to give the Company a party after the performance.

I sit between their two boxes with my 'virus'—for I am still faintly on fire with a temperature of 100°. I feel that tonight the strain on the Company is a severe one—they are acutely aware of the ordeal ahead of them.

The result of that night is well known; perhaps we shall never experience such a triumph again. The theatre was loaded with good

will, but it would not have seen us through with such a display of
tempestuous warmth if they had found us wanting. The American
has great generosity of spirit, but he would not indulge in an outburst of diplomatic politeness—he has no time and no patience with
any form of unsatisfactory soft-pedalling. What made the Company
give of their best that night was that they knew America sincerely
wished them to be worthy of success.

I missed, on that memorable opening night, one of the most unusual moments of an exciting evening.

I had gone on ahead of the Company to the Mayor's supper party,
given in the garden of his riverside residence on that sultry evening
in the first week of October. The Company were to follow in two
large buses. To get them there as speedily as possible the Mayor's
police outpost motor cyclists escorted the buses: with the sirens wailing the Sadler's Wells Ballet sped through the streets at great speed,
suspending the traffic and shooting the traffic lights. As far as the
Company was concerned it was the crowning touch of glory to the
night!

The next day we knew that the London press had taken our
success to heart and headlines greeted the New York triumph in
many British papers; I was informed later that the interest and excitement was also in evidence behind the walls of Buckingham Palace.

There is no doubt that the Hurok administration had turned all
their genius and professional sense on to the matter of presenting us
to every possible advantage. Sol Hurok is genuinely fond of artists,
and he has a staff who share, in a very human fashion, all the interests
of the firm. They work as a united family and have always displayed
understanding and kindliness towards every member of our Company—however humble might be the actual position of the artist
concerned.

New York immediately struck me as a most beautiful city. The
sharp elegance of the skyscraper is here at home—where it belongs.
It has an immense dignity in its climb towards skies that are famed
for their scintillating clarity of light; for the skyscraper, with its
delicate steel structure, that appears to grow out of space itself,

matches to perfection the cool brightness of its native skies. These structures edge the long, broad avenues—dying away in the distance into the unbroken line: New York has an endless vista of horizons—turning it into a fantasy city poised in space.

I never tire of going to the top of the Empire State building—nor do I weary of looking upwards to pick out penthouses. The penthouse is surely the American town dweller's stamp of independence; for the penthouse perches on the top or the side of the tall buildings—sometimes throwing out an oddity in roof gardens. These little houses live their own lives; they are quite independent of the rest of the city—and often wantonly out of fashion with the style of the steel triumph of engineering that supports them.

At the close of day one watches the fading light hit these great buildings, changing the planes on them, time and again, within the space of a few minutes. Sometimes the setting sun will throw one side of the city's architecture into shadow—hitting the other with the fierce blaze of its own flame-like sunset that sparkles rather than glows. One by one the windows light up; the climb of the fairy lights up into the night sky seems without end. Shortly a million stars appear to have studded the skyscrapers—filling in their façades as well as outlining their edges. You become aware of a sulphur glow that penetrates the rich night blue of the sky: the glow springs from the heart of the city's famed Broadway—Times Square. Here, with the fierce, pulsing vulgarity of every form of electric sign, one senses the native characteristics of the city . . . for Times Square might well be constructed of iridescent popcorn, viewed through a wrapping of crinkly cellophane.

As the night lights creep up the buildings that flank Central Park, I have hastened up to my bedroom window to watch the park darken under the spell of night—obscurely dark it becomes except for one spot. Suddenly *Les Patineurs* is stretched beneath me and the tiny whirling skating figures continue into the night on their illuminated skating rink that is set in the park.

New York in its varied seasons: the autumn I have seen, with Central Park every shade of brown and red—as though the clarity and iridescence of its Indian summer, and the cool penetration of its white sunlight, could not kill but just sunburn afresh all things on earth. 'The Fall' is too sad a name for this brave blaze of autumnal life: such a rich upward climb of colour to the sky obliterates from the mind the notion that there must follow the descent to leaf mould on earth. I have seen the city again under snow and the spell of Christmas. No matter if Christmas is supposed to be commercialized and its Christmas trees, that sway in its fierce winter winds, are the largest to be found . . . it will all leave you spellbound. Fantasy shop windows; Christmas wrappings that are gifts in themselves; these things mingle with the bells that chime carols, faintly heard above the roar of the traffic . . . I have stood amidst the rush of Fifth Avenue and listened to 'Holy Night'.

I have entered St. Patrick's Cathedral on an evening in Christmas week and by so doing, found myself stepping back into Europe, a Europe of the Latin and Slav *émigrés*, with their heavily sculptured, serious faces and dark, lowered eyes; their heads covered with their peasant scarves, their hands busy with the guiding of small children, or the duty of the lighted candle. I have heard here, amid the many tongues of Europe, the soft brogue of Ireland . . . and I have realized that all such people called themselves American citizens. The more you see of this side of America, the more you feel the great welding of races, ceaseless over the stretch of time from one end to the other of these mighty States.

America claims us time and again. The Company tours the States in its own train with its own orchestra and forty tons of properties. Even the train menus are headed with the name of the Ballet.

On our second visit I crossed Canada as the Company crossed the great Middle West on its way to the Pacific coast. My Canadian lecture tour of the Women's Clubs of Canada (under the auspices of the British Council) started at Ottawa and took me as far north as Edmonton and as far west as Vancouver. In twelve days I visited

eight towns. A swift memory, have I, of swooping down from the
skies at sunset to Regina, set like a round bowl in the middle of
limitless prairie. The setting sun glittered on its Congress Hall and
there was sky everywhere; I think that the great beauty of the prairie
lies in the fact that you study the sky through the changing day as
elsewhere you study the earth. Regina is some forty years old—you
are aware of circular Regina, and then, abruptly, there is prairie as
far as the eye can see. I discovered, when there, that forty women had
already chartered a plane to fly to Winnipeg in two months' time to
see the Ballet.

I remember, at the end of this lecture tour, a fantastic flight by
night down the Pacific coast—over an endless number of brilliantly
bejewelled towns—all part of a world that was outside my range of
knowledge. The Los Angeles airport, alive on a hot night with the
blaze of electric lights, seemed to be the end of all journeys from all
countries, in a world of endless journeyings.

I landed in time to witness the Company's first appearance in
Hollywood—after the success of the previous year on the East coast
. . . On the evening of the first night, as I get near the Shrine Theatre,
the sky is shot with searchlights; they dance on the thousands entering the five front entrances to this huge building. The great foyer is
packed stiff with the glitter of Hollywood . . . even the Garbo is not
noticeably alone. I give up the struggle, and trot round to the back of
the theatre, where I pick my way over packing cases and properties
to reach the stage. Our stage carpenter, Horace Fox (always, in my
mind's eye, to be seen in his ill-fitting E.N.S.A. uniform of a first
lieutenant) said to me not long ago: 'I'll always see you, madam,
that night, a'picking your way calmly through them packings and
saying—"Horace, it's a mad-house in front." '

I did not really enjoy my first visit to the States; this may have
been due to my illness which took me a year to get over. Time and
repeated visits though have given me an increasing respect and under-

standing. Always to me there is one strange contradiction—and that is the speed of their life as opposed to the speed of their thinking. . . . Yet there is nothing slow about their humour, nor are they slow to debunk—but I have wondered if this over-all mental slowness (in comparison with the European mind) is something born of a form of exhaustion, due to the high pressure of streamlined living.

The streamlined approach is a means of saving time. It may, though, curtail a certain initiative that is allied to adaptability. The American will argue that compromise points to a lack of efficiency, and this view holds much truth. One's intelligence, however, needs an occasional tweak of the tail: without exercise in the effort of living, the mind becomes as a limb that is suffering from a deficient muscular reaction.

We Europeans are time wasters: we permit an unnecessary expenditure of energy among our workers. Our tolerance towards discomfort is, time and again, inexcusable; yet it forces us to exercise some form of imaginative adjustment. The cult of speed and comfort in the States is beyond reproach, but stifles resourcefulness.

Crossing the States of America on a lecture tour I have come into contact with many sides of American life. Judged by English standards, I discovered that a high sense of comradeship, diligently cultivated, is present in their community life. In general one is aware of a great freedom-loving independent people—spread over vast lands; on closer inspection there seems to be an effort, on everyone's part, to draw closer together: a challenge perhaps to the scale of living imposed on them. Friendship, therefore, becomes a serious social obligation: there are clubs to foster every sort of interest. The women—even those whose homes are modest in comparison with those in the higher income grades—consider that they must have time away from their household chores and obligations so as to exercise their minds in many specialized directions: their houses are consequently run with a minimum of trouble and a maximum of comfort. The principle in theory is a good one; in practice it appears to have still a long way to go. There is a need for discrimination, for their mental acceptance has become too credulous: one feels that no one understands the necessity of weighing up relative values; instead there is an easy readiness to believe on very slight evidence.

The American woman at home is the antithesis of her harassed overworked British counterpart: nevertheless the latter (in spite of occasional cluckings, reminiscent of a flurried hen) has acquired the secret of craftsmanship in the running of her cold, damp and gadgetless home.

Within the American picture-frame we must place the American child: it lives in a rarefied atmosphere bestowed on it by the adult, an atmosphere charged with dedication. Spoilt is far too unsubtle a word to use: these children are a part of the streamlined preservation of the home that is so conscientiously upheld. Witness the film world as a small symbol: the English film is rarely concerned with the child (the authorities, anyway, prefer it in bed or in school), and the French film delights in portraying it as an example of original sin: thus it is left to the American film to give us the World's Sweetheart and Shirley Temple.

It is these aspects of community life among the great masses of the people, with their sudden capacity for tough thinking and doing, that spells the true America: it preserves, on the positive side, something of the root of the pioneer spirit. It is for these reasons that, for me, Mother's Day, Father's Day and similar celebrations have a deeper significance than commercialism: the business of commerce is to sense a need that can be nursed into a necessity. An American family will travel hundreds of miles to be together on Thanksgiving Day; in such cases a British family, if separated by five miles, would do nothing beyond a brief communication by telephone; nor can I imagine Father's Day in England celebrated with anything more than a humorous and faintly disrespectful postcard!

I will never cease to wonder at this New World built by the hand of man in so few pages of history . . . I will never tire of visiting the big private museums, created for the Nation by famous industrialists.

The whole approach is distinct from the historical background of the Stately Homes of England, and to me, its humility and purpose are infinitely more touching. When first in the States, I was fortunate enough to come across Carnegie's essay on 'Wealth': it was this essay that lit up my understanding of the attitude of mind behind the creation of these treasure houses.

•   •   •

These post-war years seemed to fly by swiftly—and suddenly it was the eve of our tenth anniversary in the Royal Opera House. The occasion was celebrated by the evergreen *Sleeping Beauty*.

By now the historic White Lodge, Richmond Park, had become the boarding school for the junior members of the Sadler's Wells School. The original junior school at Barons Court was handed over to the senior school, together with the newly acquired house next door, (where Nicolai Legat lived and taught in the 'twenties and 'thirties); this arrangement enabled us to rehearse both the ballet companies, if necessary, in the same building; and made it possible to keep in close contact with the top class of the senior school.

Twenty-five years ago Sadler's Wells had six dancers and some thirty students. In 1956, as I write, the two schools, two companies, and the two opera-ballet groups, number something between 350 to 400 dancers of today and tomorrow.

The post-war Sadler's Wells Theatre Ballet completed, in 1956, its first ten years of life. Its birthday coincided with the reopening of the Royal Opera House; just as the older Sadler's Wells Company shared twenty-five years of life with the rebuilt Sadler's Wells Theatre of 1931.

This younger Company grew apace from its inauguration in 1946, when the old Company moved up to Covent Garden Opera House. It has toured the States from coast to coast; it has toured Canada and South Africa and countries in Europe. It has richly served and launched our young choreographers, as it holds the early works of John Cranko, Alfred Rodrigues and Kenneth MacMillan (since then all three have produced for Covent Garden). Rising young stars of today at the Garden had all their early experience in the ten-year-old Sadler's Wells Theatre Ballet.

Nowadays there is a free exchange of artists, ballets and choreographers between the two companies: this exchange will be more obvious as the years go by, and the original accent of youth on the second Company becomes more mellowed with time: there will be a combined history that will spring from the roots of all our beginnings and our established traditions. The services today of the Sadler's Wells Theatre Ballet to the theatres of England, in the numerous towns and cities, is well known and extremely important.

It was comforting to see, on the eve of our twenty-fifth birthday, that there was already within our theatres and schools an older generation of artists who have either grown up with us, been with us from our beginning or served us for a number of years. They are now, in their turn, passing their knowledge on to the younger artists. Harold Turner, Michael Somes, John Hart, John Field; Ursula Moreton, Ailne Phillips, Pamela May, Gerd Larsen, Jill Gregory are among the more prominent who hold the custody of our English Ballet traditions. . . .

Some are abroad: Mary Skeaping at the Royal Opera, Stockholm; Alan Carter at Munich Opera House; Gordon Hamilton in Vienna; Richard Ellis in America; Celia Franca, Director of the Canadian National Ballet; they are becoming a legion, spreading in all directions.

VII

BIRTHDAY OFFERING

... 'Yesterday an Idea is Mine, today it is yours, and tomorrow it belongs to the whole world. ...'

CONSTANTIN STANISLAVSKY, *An Actor Prepares*

THE ROYAL BALLET STAFF AT THE ROYAL OPERA HOUSE
Left to right: Harold Turner, Ailne Phillips, Jill Gregory, John Hart

TURKISH
STUDENTS
AT THE
CONSERVATOIRE,
ANKARA

ARNOLD HASKELL WITH STUDENTS OF THE ROYAL BALLET SCHOOL,
WHITE LODGE, RICHMOND PARK

'BIRTHDAY
OFFERING,'
MAY 5, 1956
Left to right: Svetlana,
Beriosova, Rowena
Jackson, Elaine Fifield,
Margot Fonteyn, Nadia
Nerina, Violetta Elvin,
Beryl Grey

Photo by Roger Wood

'BIRTHDAY
OFFERING',
MAY 5, 1956

*Back row,
left to right:*
Brian
Ashbridge,
Philip
Chatfield,
Michael
Somes,
David Blair,
Desmond
Doyle

Front row:
Brian Shaw,
Alec Grant

*Photo by
Houston Rogers*

I T IS 1956 and a birthday is celebrated that coincides with the
rebirth of the Sadler's Wells Theatre—for our National Ballet is
now in its twenty-fifth year.

We shall all share in this celebration that descends on the Sadler's
Wells Ballet on its return from an American tour.

We planned big productions, but time, as always in theatrical
ventures, intervened: for once nobody expressed regret, or gave vent
to a display of marked disapproval over our postponements: it was
felt that birthday presents could wait and be presented later.

In the spring I went to Moscow, with the Royal Opera House
administrator, David Webster. Our mission was to discuss a visit to
London of the Bolshoi Theatre Ballet, an event that came to pass in
the early autumn. Our own Ballet, in return, was to round off its
birthday year by a visit to the Bolshoi Theatre at the end of November: it was to be the first Ballet Company from abroad to grace
this famous stage.

Meanwhile let us return to the spring of this same year: in March
the annual Sadler's Wells Benevolent Fund performance holds a very
special gala. The Queen, the Queen Mother and the Princess Margaret are all present; in one of the intervals Her Majesty receives
every member of the Company and staff who has served the Sadler's
Wells Ballet for twenty years.

Suddenly it is the evening of 5th May; the same night that,
twenty-five years ago, saw the Old Vic present an evening of ballet
for the first time. In those days we had guest artists and students to
supplement our regular six opera-ballet dancers.

There is just a faint similarity about yesterday and today: the number six is once again in evidence—today, though, it is six young ballerinas (Grey, Elvin, Nerina, Jackson, Beriosova, Fifield) that sweep on to the stage with their attendant swains (Chatfield, Blair, Grant, Ashbridge, Doyle, Shaw); they are led by a seventh couple—Fonteyn and Somes. Both the latter artists and the choreographer, Ashton, have seen over twenty years' service with the Sadler's Wells.

It is Frederick Ashton who has guided the leading members of the Company, during the last few weeks, towards their special appearance in *Birthday Offering*. This is a small ballet devised to the haunting music of Glazunov, arranged by Robert Irving. The gesture is a quiet one; yet it tellingly expresses twenty-five years' works in its twenty minutes of gracious choreography; all is subjected, with a sensitive intelligence, to an understanding of the individual artistry of each dancer. The work is rapturously received by the audience—for they are quick to sense something that comes from the heart as well as the head.

On each side of *Birthday Offering* there stands a stalwart member of the English Ballet repertoire: protecting as well as framing tonight's bouquets are those two balletic outposts of British Ballet produced over twenty years ago and still vitally alive—*The Rake's Progress* and *Façade*. Within these two frames we have a full length portrait of Robert Helpmann—back in his old rôles.

On this memorable night it is inevitable that the span of a quarter of a century has left some of us aware of certain losses: Lilian Baylis who once showed faith in an Idea; Constant Lambert who was one of the Idea's most important architects; Lord Keynes who did so much to further its development; Sophie Fedorovitch whose death has left it bereft of her wisdom, but nevertheless strengthened by the quietude that her memory evokes, and the visual sense of true values that her designs always awake; beautiful Pearl Argyle, whose death, just after the end of the war, took place before her English friends could end a six years' separation; Louis Yudkin, our devoted stage manager of many years, killed in an aeroplane crash in 1953. . . .

It is with mixed feelings that I look, tonight, on this Portrait of a Ballet: yet etched in firmly are the outlines of a huge organization; the detail work appears to be safe, already in the eager hands of the next generation, who, rightly enough, cannot be expected to concern themselves with the gaps that life, and its sequence of events, has made on the inroad of my personal memories.

The year moves forward: it is autumn and I am once more in America. Before I leave London I see the historic and exciting opening of the Bolshoi Ballet, setting the seal of a success that was already assured, on their long-awaited London appearance.

I have arranged to fulfil a lecture tour of the States and Canada; it is one of the many efforts to be made (in many directions) to raise funds for the Sadler's Wells School—framed in the peaceful, pastoral scene that surrounds White Lodge in Richmond Park.

I cross and recross the vast States of America, which are vibrating under the stress of the pending Presidential election . . . everywhere, again, it is faces: faces of the supporters of 'literary' clubs, who inspire me to speak of those days spent at the Abbey Theatre: I hear then the murmur of the incredulous—for here, standing in front of them, appears someone who has actually known Yeats and can speak of him and his times. William Butler Yeats is a great legendary figure amidst the literary clubs and the Universities of America. Further faces I see, belonging to the members of the Women's Clubs— earnest in their searchings are such groups, kindly in their appreciation and possibly equally forgetful of it all within a week. Lastly, the luxuriant colleges and universities: great institutions are these, set, often enough, in the heart of the countryside, that, at this precise moment, receives the fall in the full strength of its autumnal glow. Eager young girl undergraduates besiege me after the lectures, in their elegantly appointed common-rooms. I sit down: they sink to the floor in their full skirts like so many crystallized butterflies; they are crowned by their pony-tail hair fashion and wholly absorbed with their numerous questions. I sense the background of these alert young faces, so distinctive with their finely chiselled broad bone structure—it is Walt Whitman's America: I sense the responsibility of the spreading Campus far and wide, dedicated, as it is, to the sheltering of the youth of the New World in idealistic surroundings. This youth 'vibrates to a new vitality and a thirst for knowledge, a knowledge that for the moment may be a little too heady for the consumers—but still holds out so much of life and promise.

I am in Denver: it will soon be time to send a cable, some thousands of miles, to the Sadler's Wells Ballet in Moscow.

The historic cable across the world, however, was never to be sent. I find myself once more on tour—for the third time in my life I am again deeply concerned with signs of a great turmoil. I am in the Middle West and all is confusion. Suez, Hungary: threats of war challenge us from hysterical headlines in these Middle West papers— and my English accent causes curiosity in hotel and restaurant. There is nothing for me to do—in this, my own experience of isolation; I can but cling to the radio and the television for hourly news of a more world-wide order . . . for here the pending election still takes pride of place over the renewed strain and stress of Western Europe. I, who have always loved being quite alone, suddenly experience intense loneliness.

From a hotel later in Cincinnati I hear, over the telephone, David Webster tell me of the final decision to cancel the Ballet's visit to Moscow . . . he adds, though, that the Royal Charter lies on the desk—the Charter granted by Her Majesty the Queen to the two Ballet Companies and the School.

Thus they become, in this their twenty-fifth year, the Royal Ballets and the Royal School of Ballet.

Our birthday year ends with an accent on youth. The first day of 1957 sees three young English choreographers of The Royal Ballet very fully occupied. With *The Prince of the Pagodas* John Cranko has

'BIRTHDAY OFFERING' AT THE ROYAL OPERA HOUSE ON THE
NIGHT OF MAY 5, 1956

THE SADLER'S WELLS THEATRE BALLET IN THEIR TENTH
ANNIVERSARY YEAR, 1956

BIRTHDAY PORTRAIT

staged his first three-act ballet at Covent Garden—with the distinguished aid of Benjamin Britten and John Piper; Alfred Rodrigues has raised the curtain at the historic La Scala, Milan, on his version of *Casse-Noisette*—with décor and costumes by James Bailey, whose first décor was for *Giselle* at Covent Garden in 1946; young Kenneth MacMillan is in Monte Carlo; he is adding two new ballets to the repertoire of the American Theatre Ballet.

It has been said for some time that youth was knocking at the door: now they have turned the handle and walked boldly in. That is as it should be.

•   •   •

I shall return, for a moment, to the eve of our birthday year—a certain week in the end of December 1955.

I am once more in Dublin where the Sadler's Wells Theatre Ballet is fulfilling an engagement at one of the theatres. It is a damp, cold week, with the Dublin streets and pavements shining with the wet of Eire's soft relentless rain.

With my sister, who is once more living in Wicklow, I go down to Blessington to see our old home.

The years have brought many changes: to supply Dublin with water (and electricity for the grid) the Liffey has been dammed above Poulaphouca waterfalls and flooded with the King's River. There is now a gigantic lake in their respective valleys. Baltiboys is practically isolated: a vast, watery encroachment covers much of the original expansive green setting.

The changed scene has given the house a touch of lonely splendour; gone, though, is the long sheltered avenue of my childhood days, with the wood on one side steeply descending to the banks of the Liffey when (in comparison with the waters of today) it was but a wide stream . . . gone also is the lodge and the old bridge that contained a stone recording my great-great-grandfather's leap into the river on his favourite hunter—just a challenge to his horsemanship after a Hunt Supper. Gone are many familiar fields, the park and part of the gardens: they are all under this huge lake.

The countryside has now a wilder and colder beauty; this lonely, unloved-looking house, on its high ground, dominates the scene at one point—two parts surrounded as it is by water.

My sister and I go into every nook in this rambling old place—for today it is empty and once more for sale. Slightly melancholy does it seem to us in its loss of the surrounding meadows, woods, lanes and farm holdings of fifty years ago.

Inside the house we argue about the changes that the years have imposed on it—changes that make it impossible for us now to unravel all the impressions and memories of childhood. The big bell is still in its place in the yard: for sentiment's sake we try to ring it once again—across the fields I can see the home farm where I struggled with the intricacies of my Irish Jig.

The kind owners of today (who have left Baltiboys for another part of the county) have seen to our comfort on this rain-drenched day. There is a fire for us in the drawing-room, and a decanter of sherry to warm us. Shrouded in sheets, there is still a small amount of furniture in this spacious drawing-room; in sharp contrast to the bare walls a handsome Bozzi mantelpiece makes a sudden rich surrounding to the crackling fire.

Outside, everything is reminiscent of the familiar damp of long ago winter days . . . and again I hear the caw of the rooks. The lawns though have laid aside their former smooth surfaces—I cannot conjure up any vision of a green Swiss Roll. . . .

I suffer a wave of rueful despondency and in that moment I suggest that we go back to Dublin; I add that the present scene is surely becoming more and more like the last act of *The Cherry Orchard*.

"To cease upon the midnight with no pain" runs the imagery of Keats in a magic sequence of words. I feel that here, at the foot of these Wicklow Hills, lies the midnight of the first seven years of my life.

•   •   •

To belong to yesterday is neither sad nor strange—it is in the nature of things.

At the beginning of this book the Professor tells us that old age makes you feel 'stiff-like'. Baltiboys feels that way, and my Jig of the Wicklow Hills is stiffening up a bit—for over the years it has travelled quite a long way . . .

I would say that this Irish Jig, with its lively adventures, has recorded as much of its life as can be of any interest to the younger generation of Jigs that roam the wide world today.

I must not forget the reader; for he has danced with me from Blessington Fair to Covent Garden Market. It has been a lengthy journey and I thank him for his charity.

INDEX

INDEX